WORKBOOK FOR
SPIRITUAL DEVELOPMENT

WORKBOOK FOR
SPIRITUAL DEVELOPMENT

HUA-CHING NI

TAO OF
WELLNESS
PRESS

Acknowledgments: Our deep appreciation is extended to the students who assisted in editing and typesetting this book.

Published by:
Tao of Wellness Press
An Imprint of SevenStar Communications
13315 W. Washington Boulevard, Suite 200
Los Angeles, CA 90066
www.taoofwellness.com

First Printing: January 1983
Revised Edition:
      First Printing: August 1992
      Second Printing: May 1995
      Third Printing: March 2005
      Fourth Printing: September 2010

Library of Congress Cataloging-in-Publication Data

Ni, Hua-Ching.
Workbook for spiritual development of all people / by Ni, Hua-Ching.
-- 2nd ed.
    p.   cm.
   Includes index.
   ISBN 0-937064-54-8; 978-0-937064-54-2
   1. Spiritual life--Taoism. I. Title.
BL1923.N575 1992   92-13036
299'.5144--dc20   CIP

Cover Design: Justina Krakowski Design

*This book is dedicated
to those who are willing to work
on their spiritual growth every day
with unyielding determination
and constancy.*

To all readers,

According to the teaching of the Universal Integral Way, male and female are equally important in the natural sphere. This fact is confirmed in the diagram of *T'ai Chi.* Thus, discrimination is not practiced in our tradition. All of my work is dedicated to both genders of the human race.

Wherever possible, constructions using masculine pronouns to represent both sexes are avoided. Where they occur, we ask your tolerance and spiritual understanding. We hope that you will take the essence of my teaching and overlook the limitations of language. Gender discrimination is inherent in English. Ancient Chinese pronouns do not differentiate gender. I wish that all of you will achieve yourselves well above the level of language and gender.

Thank you, H. C. Ni

Warning - Disclaimer

This book is intended to present information and techniques that have been in use throughout the Orient for many years. This information and these practices utilize a natural system within the body; however, no claims are made regarding their effectiveness. The information offered is according to the author's best knowledge and experience and is to be used by the reader at his or her own discretion and liability.

Because of the sophisticated nature of the information contained within this book, it is recommended that the reader also study the author's other books for a broader understanding of energy-conducting exercises and a healthy lifestyle.

People's lives have different conditions and their growth has different stages. Because the background of people's development cannot be unified, there is no single practice that can be universally applied to everyone. Thus, it must be through the discernment of the reader that the practices are selected. The adoption and application of the material offered in this book must therefore be the reader's own responsibility.

The author and publisher of this book are not responsible in any manner for any harm that may occur through following the instructions in this book.

Contents

List of Figures

Prelude

The Universal Way is the destination
   of all spiritual efforts of humankind.
It serves all people's lives,
   everywhere and always.

The Universal Way conveys the deep truth
   of all conscious elaborations
   of the human mind.
It contains the vast and profound essence
   of the human spirit.
Thus it transcends all religions,
   leaving them behind,
   like the clothing of a bygone season.

The Universal Way is the goal of all sciences,
   but is not locked at the level of the mind.
It cuts through all skepticism
   and inexhaustible searching.
Thus it surpasses all sciences,
   leaving them behind,
   like historical relics of the past.

The Subtle Essence that is sought
   by all sciences and all religions
   transcends all attempts to reach it
   by means of thought, belief or experiment.
The Universal Way leads directly to it
   and guides you to reach it yourself by uniting
   with the integral nature of the universe.

The Universal Way is like the master key
   to all doors leading to the inner room
   of ultimate truth.
It is the master teaching of all teachings,
   yet it relies on no religion or experiment.
There is no need for intellectual or emotional detours
   that cannot serve the lives of all people
   everywhere and always.
Follow the Universal Way beyond all boundaries
   to the heart and essence of natural life itself.

Preface

Dear friends, most spiritual endeavors are merely
emotional or psychological games. In general, religious
rituals are defined as worship, but truthfully they are either
emotional demands or psychological needs which have
prevailed since ancient times. More than half of today's
population still continue to play these emotional games and
still need their emotional security blankets to support their
lives.

Life is wide and varied, and different circumstances call
for different kinds of support. Religious beliefs and activities
can be an important means of traversing the great path of
life, but it still takes correct guidance and courage.
Unfortunately, most religions are nothing more than social
institutions and do not provide much opportunity for
individual growth. Few people know exactly what their
religious activities mean, but even so, their effect is
widespread.

Another category of spiritual endeavor is the result of
personal spiritual effort and development and is not socially
supported at all. Without a total investment of your energy,
no spiritual development can be reached. Therefore, the first
thing you must understand about this book is that there are
no emotional games and no psychological crutches. It
contains only pure spiritual practices for the spiritual
development of people who have already made major
emotional, psychological and conceptual breakthroughs. If
you are still wandering around in the muck and mire of
personal confusion, you might want to read some of my other
books first. They were written to help those who are working
on clarity of mind and spirit and the purification of all kinds
of confusion.

Personal spiritual development is not something that
comes from someone else's charity or kindness. It is a solely
personal endeavor. There is no way you can transfer your
development to your loved ones as you can with material
wealth. You can teach and show others the direction and

practices to follow, but you cannot transfer your achievement or development itself, not even to your own son or daughter.

Cutting through your emotional problems, mental conceptions and personal life problems provides the possibility to restore personal balance and poise. Once you have this foundation, the next step will be easy. The simple spiritual practices in this book are intended to help anyone who is looking for what to do in order to develop spiritually and integrally. There is not much here to talk or think about. The value of this book is not in its words, but rather in the use of its contents and the harvest of its practices.

Developed people have already come to a stage where they can take advantage of social improvements. The dominance of a religion or social custom does not really influence them. They have the freedom which makes a proper foundation for personal spiritual achievement.

The freedom that some modern people have achieved is like the beginning of the world when there was no organized social system and people had time to work on their spiritual achievement. However, people are now bound to their self-created systems and have so embalmed themselves in narrow political doctrines or religious beliefs that their life decisions are determined by some external authority rather than by their own search for the truth.

Fortunately, some people have awakened from religious backwardness and can offer their energy to support the spiritual development. They do not let narrow mindedness or shortsightedness become decisive factors in their individual development. In the last thirty years, after a bitter taste of the destruction of war, religious and technological breakthroughs in Western society have brought opportunities for all people to study, without the interference of religious dominance, the total achievement of human beings in all generations.

Once you attain personal self-integration, you can recognize other integral beings. For people who are still developing, the problem is not only to believe, but to be the truth. I hope that developed people will help to dissolve all dark and unvirtuous controls over other humans. With the awakening and spiritual development of more individuals, those controls

will no longer affect our lives or cause further war and
conflict.

If you are satisfied with the peace you reach, then do not
disturb or obstruct other people's achievement, for their
achievements are valid also. The fundamental, central path
of human spiritual development is not to look for
psychological or emotional peace in a limited way, but rather
to look for the truth itself. All understandable truth is
discussed in my other books, but this workbook is a tool that
is to be used differently. In order to build a better and
stronger foundation, I recommend that you first read my
other books so that this book will be more useful. It is
designed to assist your personal spiritual maturity and
development. Each word, especially in the invocations,
displays the inner beauty and integrity of your life being in
which you are the center of the universe. The reality is you
and your spiritual projection and connection.

Since the beginning, no other teacher of the natural
truth has written and spoken out more than I. These works
are my response to the drastic changes and challenges of the
modern world. This is a time when all natural spiritual
knowledge has been lost due to religious dominance and tha
incomplete development of science. The problems of
mankind are greater and deeper today than at any other time
in history. My books are an attempt to help your spiritual
growth.

This is my sixth year of service here in the United
States. I hope I have been of positive assistance to the
spiritual development of all people. The knowledge I offer no
longer belongs to a single spiritual tradition, family or
person, but to all humans and to the universe. I offer such
spiritual wealth to all who can use it. The cornerstone of
correct self-cultivation is, "All the highest things start from
what is fundamental."

Hua Ching Ni
January 1, 1984
Los Angeles, California
U.S.A.

Chapter 1

A Workbook
for Your Spiritual Development

How This Book Will Serve You

It is burdensome to be a human being. Why? Because there is a lot to learn and a lot to be experienced in the process of personal growth. No life, especially human life, can escape personal growth. Therefore, it is helpful to learn what is most serviceable and essential to life.

You may ask what is most essential in the life of a human being. I would say it is life itself. In human life, all of us have three spheres: physical, mental and spiritual. It cannot be denied that all life needs material support, but our entire life being is not limited only to the material sphere. Our spirit also needs development. The direction of human society, however, has changed radically from the pursuit of spirit to the pursuit of the material. In today's overpopulated modern world, material and mental aspects of life are overemphasized, especially in the form of intellectual knowledge which makes people deny even the existence of a spiritual level of life, much less recognize its importance.

People need spiritual growth and development to be whole, but they take a partial view of life as the result of advances in scientific research and industrial technology which disregard the whole scope of human life. We cannot use the same methods that apply to material discoveries to explore the spiritual sphere. Many people are disappointed and deny the existence of a spiritual realm because they never see the error of using the wrong tools.

Interestingly enough, some advanced scientists who are experts and leaders in their fields have good spiritual energy. Although you cannot find any hint of spirit in the presentation of their theories, behind their discoveries and contained in their cosmologies is good spiritual energy which happens to be expressed through great material discoveries and inventions. These scientists have put all of their energy - physical, mental, spiritual - into one thing, and through that wholeness of being have accomplished great things. Originally, all people were integral beings, and if someone worked on something, all three spheres were involved in the process. Usually when we do something we are usually fragmented. Our body does one thing, and our mind is thinking about something else.

People have been misguided by new material discoveries and technological developments and have used them as reasons to deny the spiritual sphere of life. This is a great mistake. Our political leaders also gather their impressions from scientific research and deny the existence of divinity with assertive authority. It is easy to make assertions about the world or life without careful research or deep exploration. It is more difficult to prove the truth of something step by step.

What we call the spiritual path is really the common education of basic life. Modern education works only on the physical and mental levels; it avoids spiritual matters and does not support spiritual development, obviously neglecting the most essential part of life. We must realize that spiritual development is not only the work of religion, but of everyone. It is the work of the schools to teach the fundamental principles of individual development. Many outstanding citizens are active socially, politically, and financially, but they cannot do anything on the spiritual level. Why? Because they cover their spiritual eyes and cannot see the truth. People make religion responsible for their spiritual development in the same way they make physicians responsible for their health, and insurance companies responsible for their security. That is not the correct way of going about life. True responsibility still rests with the individual, and the entire being and development of the person are involved.

This book addresses itself to all three realms of development. The material presented here cannot be found in general education. Why? Because in general education today such fundamental and useful things as common sense and a basic knowledge of human life are not seen as valuable. Modern education teaches only those things that make people superficially knowledgeable. Thick books may help you get high grades, but they are not necessarily helpful when you enter life. I often see many intellectual people, professors or professionals, who have no common sense about themselves or others. It is not their fault. It is the fault of modern tendencies that cover their eyes and blind them to what is important in their lives. This is why I am interested in contributing this book to all lovers of a natural life of complete development.

Spiritual development must deepen and explore the truth in order for a person to achieve the goal of integralness, step by step. This takes years and depends entirely on how the person receives their spiritual education and works on himself or herself. This is the foundation of individual spiritual development. It is a personal matter, never one of mass production.

The teaching of Tao originated in prehistoric times. For many generations people searched out methods by which to develop themselves. These methods are numerous and some have even been formalized as different schools which emphasize one or two things and make other aspects secondary to one's personal cultivation. Here I would like to give you some idea of the many effective methods which are practiced among achieved ones.

Nei Tan, 内丹 , Internal Medicine, which can support a person's spiritual future through refinement of the physical, mental and spiritual essence; Tai Shi, 胎息, Internal Breathing, which is higher than external breathing, although both are usually practiced together; Tao Yin, 導引 Energy Channeling, for purposes of health and spiritual benefit; Chun Shih, 存思, , Visualization or concentration; Fu Erh, 服餌, External Nutrition, using natural herbs and other things; Shing Jeau, 行蹻, Walking, for gathering and refining energy; Fuh Chi, 伏氣 , Internal Energy Maintenance; Bei Gu, 辟穀, to stop eating food completely (especially helpful to those who are cultivating spiritually so that they can stop looking for and preparing food for themselves - eventually they combine their life with the environment); Fu Chi, 服氣, Intaking Natural Energy through Breathing and Swallowing, which should be practiced with Bei Gu; Fang Jung, 房中 , Sexual Cultivation; Fu Jyeo, 符咒 , Secret Talismanic Characters, Words, and also Invocations; Jing

Tan, 金丹 , Golden Elixir; Shr Jeah, 尸解 , Method of
Exuviation into a New Life.

There are many others, but this will give you some idea
of how many different methods were developed for the
purpose of achieving spiritual development. In a system-
atized spiritual practice, there are essentially three
approaches. The first is called *Tai Ching*, in which people
work through discipline in the pursuit of virtuous fulfillment. Maintenance of health is also included in this path.
The second path is that of *Sang Ching*, or pure spiritual
practice. The third is the path of *Yu Ching*, in which the
person achieves through wisdom and enlightenment. These
three paths represent the different ways of reaching spiritual
development. Some reach through physical development,
others reach through the mind and mental practices, and
still others search through wisdom and enlightenment. In
this book the methods recommended are all interconnected,
because it is difficult to isolate one category by itself. There
are other methods which I have mentioned in other books,
but the purpose of this book is to concentrate on your
personal spiritual development.

Anyone who carefully works with this and my other
books, without taking a partial approach, will be safe and
will benefit in their spiritual achievement. If you take my
offerings as a whole, not in part, you shall have a good
harvest. If you are still at the stage of looking for a broad
understanding of spiritual matters, this is not the book you
need. My earlier books were written for that purpose. To
whomever uses this book as a tool for his or her own
spiritual development, my blessing is given to you daily.
Through working step by step and uniting with the spirits of
thousands and thousands of achieved spiritual beings, you
will surely achieve yourself.

A Whole Person

A whole person is not a new idea or an idealistic way of being, a whole person is simply a natural being. If we look at the balanced life of a natural being, half of it would be external and half would be internal. Without the momentary events of external life, how could we distinguish spiritual eternity? It is all one thing. How do you express your spiritual centeredness? By experiencing all the events and things in life without being especially internally or externally directed. Spiritual people may be more inward for purposes of personal development, but one must find the right time and way to serve the external world and express the wholeness of life.

On the scale of self-cultivation, we say that the body, mind and spirit can be equally valued, cultivated, and developed. High spiritual achievement develops from physical essence, with the mind as the medium between the physical and spiritual spheres. Its duty is to organize a harmonious state of music through a beautiful life. In the sense of personal responsibility, to be a whole person means that if you do a job, you do your best. You cannot be a 50% or 60% person, you have to do your best, 100%. This does not mean to exhaust yourself, it just means that anything you do is your personal expression of wholeness.

As to negative things, do not involve any part of your being, not even one single percent, with them. They will only harm your wholeness and completeness. If it is your personal goal to become a whole person, this is practical advice. In your everyday life, check yourself out and see if you are step by step furthering yourself toward physical, mental and spiritual achievement and integration. Since your greatest essence is spirit, use the physical and mental to obey the spiritual in order to reach wholeness. This means that it is the subtle element which is the true lord. No whole person can be a bad person. A whole person is a balanced and positive person. This is only the outline of a whole being in union with the ultimate Tao.

Chapter 2

Work to Improve
Your Understanding

The Ancient Achieved Ones:
Important Models of Complete Unification

The True Value of a Teacher Is his Personal Being

There was a simple man from the state of Lu named Wang Tai who was a teacher without a platform, but who had as many followers as Confucius. One day Chang Chi, a student of Confucius, asked him, "Wang Tai, whose followers in the state of Lu are equal in number to yours, neither preaches nor engages in discussion, yet after going to him knowing nothing, one returns filled to fullness. Is there really such a thing as formless instruction which can lead the mind to wholeness? What sort of man is he?"

Confucius replied, "He is a sage, and I have been tardy in visiting him, but I intend to make him my teacher and encourage others to do the same. Not just in the state of Lu, but I will lead the whole world to his feet."

The student asked, "He seems like an ordinary creature, yet you intend to make him lord over you. He must certainly be far above average! In what unique way does he utilize his mind?"

Confucius replied, "Honor and disgrace, life and death, are indeed big things, but they have no effect upon him. Even if Heaven and Earth were to fall in ruins he would not lose himself in the chaos. He clearly sees the truth of life and so does not shift with the change of things, but holds fast to the source."

"What do you mean?" the student asked.

"If you look at things from the point of view of superficial differences, they all appear to be different: liver and gall, people and their lands, the State of Chu and the State of Yueh, etc. However, if you look at them at their root, there is sameness. The myriad things are all one. A man such as Wang Tai does not follow what his ears or eyes prefer; he keeps his mind in harmony with virtue, seeing things as a unity, not seeing defects or loss. Even with all the facts at his disposal, he uses his conscience to command his mind, which reaches the constancy of Universal Mind. Why should he be held in such high esteem for this? "No one uses flowing water as a mirror, only still water is reflecting. Only the still can still the search for stillness. Of the things deriving their life from the earth, pine and cypress trees are models of steadiness, for they are green in summer and winter. Of those who receive their life from Heaven, Niao (reign 2357-2258 B.C.) and Shun (reign 2257-2208 B.C.), two emperors who fulfilled their public service with a humble spirit and also achieved themselves internally) are models of virtuousness and rectitude, for they were able to keep their lives on the right path and set a good example for others.

"In order to preserve originalness, one should be like the fearless soldier in battle who bravely fights for honor. In the same manner, those who have deeply recognized the core of nature can attain fearlessness by presiding over their sensory faculties and reaching for deathlessness of spirit. Such a one chooses the day to ascend. Those of high understanding come to follow such a one, but such a person has no need to gather people around him."

The Virtue of Naturalness and Simplicity

Among the students of Lao Tzu there was one called Geng Sang Tzu. He learned the natural path from his teacher and later moved to the mountain of Steep Cliff to live by himself. He had followers, but as he practiced the natural path, the clever ones left him along with the students and attendants who preferred artificial teachings. Only those men and women of simple and innocent minds came to follow him, live with him and place themselves under his guidance and instruction. After three years, the community on the mountain of Steep Cliff became prosperous and enjoyed a good harvest. The people of Steep Cliff talked among themselves and said, "When Master Geng Sang first came we were all surprised at the lack of difference between him and us. Now three years have passed. If we were to calculate what we made each day, it would not be enough, but if we were to calculate what we made each year, we have something left over. Therefore, Master Geng Sang must be a sage. Why not make him king to govern the nation?" Geng Sang Tzu heard this when he was sitting with his face to the south and he was displeased with what he heard. His students observed this, and Geng Sang said to them, "All of you think I am special. The soft warm breeze of spring and the ripening climate of autumn are the results of a natural cycle. No one has to do anything about them. I learned from Lao Tzu that the highly developed one living in an ordinary place is not recognized by most people, and they do not know what can be learned from him. That is natural. The people of Steep Cliff wish to idolize me. This makes me wonder if I am doing what Lao Tzu taught me."

The students said, "We think differently. A narrow stream is for small fish, not big fish. To respect a virtuous one by giving him a high position has been done since Niao and Shun were Emperors. The people of Steep Cliff wish to follow this custom. We wish you to accept their offer."

Geng Sang Tzu said, "Come all of you and listen to me. To establish kings and emperors is unnatural, because it places someone above other people. It is artificial and immoral. Someone may be born wiser than others, but not higher in position. Position is the result of artificial human intrusion. People will then seek the favor of the special ones, and scheming and contention will happen. To raise someone and establish them has created many disturbances in the long course of human history. It is all unnecessary. Such institutions are like the growth of a sixth finger on one's hand. They are of no use to human life. The principle of governing the world is the same as governing the individual human body. Too much interference is harmful to its growth and health. People need to know how to maintain their lives as organically as they can, including the necessary establishment of society. I value organic life. I do not value artificial positions.

"Monkeys need to stay in trees; otherwise no matter how big they are, there is danger of being caught. Fish need to stay in water; otherwise no matter how large they get, they can be humiliated by tiny ants. A person who values life needs to stay away from artificial traps. Those artificial cultural leaders and authorities are unworthy of admiration. Their ambition to reorganize the order of the world according to their imagination is like destroying the wall that serves as a fence for plants or like counting rice instead of cooking it. Once artificial standards and values are established, then people reject each other. Hypocrisy becomes the fashion. People lose their naturalness and originalness. They rush after artificial profits and thus, sons may kill fathers and subjects may kill the king. Violence perseveres under beautiful names. Even in the light of day people destroy the houses of others for 'fashionable' radical ideologies. I tell you, the source of all worldly troubles now and for thousands of years to come is that people prey upon other people through abuse of intellect, with its distortions and confusion. They have established institutions with no healthy balance or consciousness of natural morality."

Truth Has No Age

His student, Nan Jung Chu, heard this with fear and said, "As old as I am now, with so much worldly experience and learning, how am I to return to the natural way?"

Geng Sang Tzu said, "Keep your physical shape well. Maintain your innate nature. Do not let your mind run after all kinds of things all the time. After three years you may return to your original naturalness and regain the trueness of your being."

Nan Jung Chu said, "Although the shape of people's eyes are all the same, some eyes cannot see certain colors. And although the shape of people's ears are all the same, some vibrations of sound cannot be picked up by all ears. People's brains may not differ in shape, but some people cannot manage themselves well. Now you instruct me to 'return to my nature.' It is like telling the blind to look, or the deaf to listen. There is a separation between the blind and the deaf and the object. I do not know how it is possible in my case."

Geng Sang Tzu said, "As the saying goes, worker bees have no power to transform into butterflies, and the little hens of Yu cannot hatch the egg of a swan, but there is still the possibility for you to learn. My capability cannot help you, but you may go to the South to see Lao Tzu."

The Unity Between Interior and Exterior Beings

Thus Nan Jung Chu took some dry food with him and traveled for seven days and seven nights to reach the place where Lao Tzu lived. Lao Tzu said to him, "Do you come from where Geng Sang Tzu lives?"

"Yes sir," answered Nan Jung Chu.

"Why do you come with so much luggage behind you?" asked Lao Tzu.

Nan Jung Chu was surprised by this question and turned his head to look back. Lao Tzu continued, "Do you understand what I have said?"

Nan Jung Chu felt ashamed and hung his head, and then looked up with a sigh and said, "Now I forget how to answer you and what I came to ask!" He had truly brought too many unnecessary belongings with him: a mind full of useless thoughts and conceptions.

"What do you wish to ask?" said Lao Tzu.

"I have three questions which trouble me, thus I wish to obtain your instruction. Please help me for the sake of Master Geng Sang. My questions are: 1) If I keep myself unlearned, I am called ignorant. If I extend myself in learning, then to know more is to worry more; 2) To be unkind would be to harm others, but to be kind and nice I may be harmed; 3) To be unfair and unrighteous would harm others, but to be fair and righteous would harm myself. Thus I do not know how to be myself."

Lao Tzu said, "I already know your mind from your eyebrows. You look like a small child who has lost his parents. You want to probe the big sea with a rod. You have gone astray and want to restore your true nature, but you do not know how. It is sad."

Nan Jung Chu begged to stay in the guest house. He worked to restore the sense of what he truly loved and forsook the sense of what he truly disliked. He thought he was being true to himself, but after ten days he started to worry so he visited Lao Tzu again.

Lao Tzu said, "Cleanse your mind, and essential harmonious energy will grow within you. Now, small puzzles and perplexities still bother you. Let me show you the way. "When your eyes and ears are tempted by sound and color, do not try to control the disturbance. Never use the mind to stop the confusion of the eyes and ears. When your mind is bound by desire for external things, do not try to control them by any method. In a case like this, people of high moral achievement cannot keep themselves well, so how can one of imitation do so?"

Nan Jung Chu said, "Great sir, the sick need strong medicine. What I need is the way to maintain my health. Thus I wish to learn only the way of keeping my innate nature whole."

Lao Tzu said, "If you wish to know the fundamental way of protecting your innate nature or original human nature, first you must inspect yourself and not deviate from the original pristine nature. Can you free your nature from imitating worldly people? Can you know the correct and peaceful rule which tells good fortune and misfortune without using any method of divination? Can you be happy and self-content with what you are? Can you restrain yourself from rushing after external satisfaction? Can you keep from imitating artificial cultural and religious concepts and develop your pure essence? Can you not be bound by anything? Can you harmonize with the surroundings without losing your own nature? Can you have the heart of a small baby? Look at the baby, so full of life. It does not become hoarse from a whole day of crying. It does not use some of its organs and not others, but exercises its whole body. It holds its palm with the fingers coiled inward. It expresses the nature of wholeness. It looks around all day with untiring eyes. Its vitality is expressed, but it is not totally outgoing. It moves without knowing why and where. It stays without knowing the purpose of staying. It is flexible with its surroundings, like water following the currents.

"A baby can fully enjoy its life without any need to learn from somebody. This is called natural. One who learns from the baby is a student of life. One who learns from artificial doctrines is a student of death. To learn more is to lose more. To be more natural is to enjoy more of life. This is the fundamental path of life which stays uninvolved with the changing external world."

Nan Jung Chu asked, "Are these the virtues of the most highly developed one?"

Lao Tzu answered, "No, they still are not. That state is like a piece of ice that has melted. Even the cold has disappeared. The natural life of a baby is instinctive. It is outside the comprehension of nature. The most highly achieved one leads his life practically and is well-grounded in the Earth. He also enjoys his spiritual freedom with Heaven. He is not disturbed by the conflicts of people or things. He does not make people feel strange around him, nor does he feel strange around them. He never joins any planning. He never commits himself to any worldly task. He moves with complete freedom. This is how the most highly developed one leads his life."

Nan Jung Chu asked, "Is this the highest achievement?"

"Not yet," Lao Tzu replied. "But take the advice I have just given you. Be like a baby. A baby does not separate its mind from its actions. Its being is as natural as a piece of untouched wood. There is not the slightest hint of any sort of good fortune or misfortune connected with it."

The Integral One

Lei Tzu said to Kuan Yuan, "The integral, virtuous person is not harmed when he walks under water, nor does he become hot when walking on fire. He does not fear walking through anything. I beg to know how to achieve this level."

Kuan Yuan said, "One achieves this level by maintaining harmonious energy and cultivating calm-mindedness. It is not cleverness, skill, resolution or bravery that makes a person capable of such things. Come, sit down and let me tell you.

"All things with form, visibility, color and sound are physical. No physical thing can be superior to any other physical thing. How can one rise above all things of form? By separating oneself from the level of discrimination of sound, color, and so forth, one can reach the state of preformation. If this state can be attained and the great truth of it understood, one will not be controlled by external things. One will not touch any boundaries. Life is enjoyed within the territory of balance and harmony. One embodies within oneself the supernatural path of no beginning and no end. The mind swims in the original state before the development of the universe. One's true nature is kept intact and pure. The vital *chi* is cultivated. One protects oneself with subtle virtue and applies the rules of the creator, not the created. One is full of life and whole with spiritual energy. No external things can enter one's innermost sacred house. No shock enters the mind of one who is converged with the spirit. In case of friction with external things, one experiences no panic. Because the integral person assimilates nature, external things cannot be harmful.

"Do not use your intelligence to search for the true nature of things, but follow your true nature to harmoniously join with nature; thus one subtly unites with the high morality which shows no partiality. Once people apply their intelligence to planning, managing and scheming, their innate nature is damaged. True spiritual leadership never goes against what is natural, nor does it adopt what is artificial, thus people can return to their true being."

Purification of the Mind

Yen Hwei asked, "How do we learn to assist people who wish to learn the Integral Way?"

The teacher replied, "In order to learn to accomplish a virtuous mission one must not rush out and push his ideas on people. One needs to prepare oneself through self-purification. To apply one's preconceptions to a task does not attain the goal; one becomes critical and creates unnecessary obstruction. In so doing, he is unable to see the truth of things."

Yen Hwei asked, "I have kept myself sober and eaten no flesh of any kind. Can this be considered purification?"

The teacher answered, "This is only sacrifice. It is not the essence of purification."

Yen Hwei asked, "What is the essence of purification? I beg to know."

The teacher replied, "You begin by concentrating on the ears. Do not listen with the faculty of hearing, but with your mind. What ears can hear is meaningless sound. Then listen, not with your mind, but with your energy. What the mind can hear is changeable phenomena. Only *chi* does not objectify things, but is receptive to all. Then there is only the true path which exists in the great void. To be empty-minded is the essence of purification."

Yen Hwei asked, "When I had not received the precious guidance of 'the purification of the mind' I solidly felt my own existence. After receiving this guidance, I do not feel my existence. Is this empty-mindedness or the void?"

The teacher answered, "This is the essence of the 'purification of the mind.' Let me advise you, when you encounter a difficult situation, you must remain flexible. Hold no preconceptions in the mind. Do not be stirred by fame or wealth. Do not make people listen to you. Do not give people a chance to make you a target for attack. Handle everything according to the exact demand of the circumstance. This is close to the true path.

"It is easy to not apply the true path in doing things. It is not easy to leave no trace in applying the true path in doing things.

"It is easy to become hypocritical under the pressure of friendship and love. It is hard to be hypocritical under the pressure of nature.

"With wings, things can fly. With wisdom, one can comprehend the high practices. Look at the creative and responsive void of the universe. Blessings stay in quiet empty spaces. If a person is busy-minded, it is like trying to sit while you run. If one abandons the mind, the will, knowledge and intelligence to reach the inner spirit, then divine spiritual beings come to stay, not to mention human beings. This is the law of harmonizing changing phenomena. Sagacious emperors such as Fu Shi, the Yellow Emperor, Niao, Yu, Shun and those who came before them all followed this, as did the developed ones among the people."

Rediscover Your Unconfined Original Nature

Chu Chueh Tzu, an ancient wise man, said to Chang Wu Tzu, an ancient sage, "I have heard that an integral one does not interfere in secular affairs. He does not greedily run after profit and acclaim or engage in endless pursuits. Nor does he attempt to hide from trouble. He does not value what worldly people value. He does not purposely establish his teaching, though he may teach. His spirit roams beyond the narrow scope of the muddiness of worldly life. People may think this is crazy talk, but I think it is the true path of life. What do you think?"

Chang Wu Tzu answered, "This high teaching has not been heard even by wise emperors, how can it be reached by most people? Beware, my young friend. Do not hurriedly think you have attained it. This is like seeing an egg and asking for the chicken, or seeing the arrow and asking for the well-cooked game.

"Let me add something to what you have heard, in case you need it. Keep the sun and the moon as your company and embrace the entire universe in order to embody oneness. The integral one remains undisturbed by the overwhelming confusion and darkness of the world. He treats the mean and noble as one and the same. While people busily crowd together, the integral one looks like a simpleton and knows nothing. Yet he encompasses the boundless changes of billions and billions of years, and thus attains the realm of highest purity. All things follow the path of great evolution; from the One comes the natural process of compiling, then fermenting, refining and eventually returning back to the One.

"Knowing this, one who remains attached to a particular perplexity, or to their fear of transforming the coarseness of life, is like someone who is lost in a strange country, not knowing how to return home."

The Abuse of Intelligence

The true path is simple. It cannot be practiced in conjunction with anything else. Once one applies a mixed way, confusion comes. Confusion becomes the source of disaster, and then things are beyond remedy. The most developed ones in ancient times first made themselves stand firm, then they gave assistance to others. If one does not stand firm, then how can he support others?

How does virtue become corrupted? Through the abuse of intelligence. Virtue becomes corrupted because of the desire for renown. The abuse of intelligence also comes about through competition. Name and position become sources of friction and conflict. Intelligence becomes the tool of contention. These ways cannot be the rules of one's behavior.

If a person of deep virtue is not known, he does not need to compete for recognition. The worst thing is to show off with words, making other people lower than oneself. This is to devalue people. People will inevitably do something in turn to devaluate such a person. This is not the way of a person of deep virtue.

The Most Developed One

Nei Chueh asked Wang Ni, "Sir, do you know the universal truth of all things?"

Wang Ni replied, "Why should I know that?"

Nei Chueh asked, "Sir, do you know yourself?"

Wang Ni replied, "Why should I know that?"

Nei Chueh asked, "Then should all lives know nothing?"

Wang Ni replied, "Why should I know that? However, I will ask you this. How can you know that what I say I do not know is not what I know? And how can you know what ordinary people say they know is not what they do not know?

"Let me also ask you, if a man sleeps where it is wet, he becomes sick and maybe paralyzed as well, but how about an eel? Again, a man will shake in panic at the top of a tall tree, but how about a monkey? Among all three, can you tell which is the right place for each of them?

"Men eat meat and vegetables. Deer eat grass. Centipedes are fond of the brains of snakes. Owls and crows feast on decayed rats. What would be a delicious dinner for all of them?

"Deer make love, and so do birds and fish. Yet, when the most beautiful, desirable woman comes too close, fish hide, birds fly away, and deer run. What can you say is beauty for all? Thus you can see the artificial standards of human society; the conventional wisdom of humanity decides what is right and wrong, but only creates confusion and distortion. Why should I diverge from the true nature?"

Nei Chueh said, "You may not know to value the truth of benefit or harm, but the most developed one does."

Wang Ni said, "The most developed one has reached the highest magnificence. He is the one whom fire cannot make hot, nor the frozen river make cold, nor the sudden shaking of the mountain or overturning ocean shock. Such a one rides in a carriage of clouds, with the Sun and the Moon for wheels, and roams in the realm beyond the four sides of the water. The changes of life and death can do nothing to disturb him, nor do they benefit him."

True Freedom

Chuang Tzu was traveling on a mountain and he saw a huge tree with luxuriant branches and leaves. The tree had not been touched by the woodcutter and Chuang Tzu asked him why he had not cut it. The woodcutter replied, "Although this tree is big, it is of no use." Chuang Tzu said to his students who followed him on his trip, "Because that tree is the wrong kind of material, it is of no use and thus it is saved."

Then they left the mountain to stay at a friend's home. The friend was happy at this surprise visit and ordered his servant to kill one of the geese to treat his guests. The young servant asked which one of the geese would be killed and the host answered, "The one which cannot sing."

The next day one of Chuang Tzu's students asked him, "Yesterday the tree on the mountain was spared for its uselessness and thus enjoyed the long years nature allotted it. Yet our host killed the useless goose which could not sing, so where does safety lie?"

Chuang Tzu replied, "There is a fine line between being useful and useless. That sounds like it is the path, but eventually it is not, because it is still under someone else's dominion or command. The true path is to dissolve oneself within the universal harmonious order. Then one can enjoy freedom from the material realm.

"When one reaches the true path he forgets praise or disgrace or jeering comments. He moves or keeps still according to the variation of the time and circumstance. He does not insist on personal opinions, nor does he take sides. Whenever he is pulled down or flies high he always follows the principle of harmonizing himself with what is most universal. Thus he keeps his spirit in the high realm of pre-Heaven. He uses external things to serve life, and thus is not enslaved by them. Then how can he be burdened? This was the doctrine of Shen Nung and the Yellow Emperor.

"The material sphere of the world and the human realm are different. If there is a meeting, there must be a departure. If there is accomplishment, there must be deterioration. The pure and clean invite scandal. The respectable and noble suffer attachment. Positive work can draw bad comments. The virtuous can be persecuted. The unvirtuous can go unpunished. How can one take a stand among these! Such is the unhappiness of the human world! Remember, dear students, there is only one way to enjoy true freedom. True freedom exists only in the highest sphere of the Integral Realm."

The Path of Subtle Integration

Referring to Lao Tzu, Chuang Tzu said, "My Master said that the path of subtle integration encompasses both large and small things. Thus it can be everything; the variety of all things are only the tips of its branches. Only the most developed one can enjoy its simple essence.

"If the most developed one assumes the leadership of the world, though the responsibility is heavy, it is not a burden to him. All people under Heaven may fight for power, but he keeps himself aloof and maintains his independence. He knows the reality behind all things but does not change it for profit or desire. He attains the truth of all things and keeps to the simple origin. Therefore, he can surpass Heaven and Earth, and forget all things. With no disturbance to his spirit, he follows the path of subtle integration.

He embodies great virtue. He does not hold in high regard the minor teachings of love and justice. He is beyond the enjoyment of music and dance. This is because in his heart is the most precious and subtle path which makes him independent."

The Indefinable Pure Realm

At the beginning of the universe there is nothing. It cannot be called by any name. It is neither spirit nor matter, but is above everything. It originates itself. From the natural creative virtue of the indefinable oneness, all things and lives have their origin. Before anything and any life was formed, the flow of *yin* and *yang* naturally merged, but they were also distinct. Their division creates the sense of "destiny." Through the interaction of the basic patterns of energy *yin* and *yang*, different forms of life are produced.

All lives with form embody spirit, which has the subtle function of seeing, hearing, talking and moving with or without apparent organs. This is called "nature." The developed one cultivates nature and thereby returns to the realm of virtue. The highest state of virtuous achievement unites with the beginning of the universe and enters the Pure Realm.

The Pure Realm is the center of the great path of subtle integration. Nothing is excluded from it. The developed one lives a life of no personal demands. He is like the songs of birds; he is the song of nature. No one else can sing his song. Thus the developed one's life is in consonance with universal life. There is no trace of separation between the individual and the great whole. He is self-dissolving, merging into the great universal life. This is called "subtle virtue" which assimilates the great naturalness of all things.

The Mind of Wholeness

Chuang Tzu said, "My teacher, Lao Tzu, said that the Integral Truth is what covers and supports all things. It is overwhelming. People must give up all their preconceptions or they can never experience and understand this subtle truth.

"Here are ten qualities to be included in a developed mind. 'Heavenliness' means to do things without a selfish motive. 'Virtuousness' means to say things without preoccupation. 'Humility' means to love people universally. 'Greatness' means to look at different things as sharing the same body with oneself. 'Broadness' means to behave with unlimited flexibility. 'Richness' means to enjoy the differences of all things. 'Orderliness' means to deal with things no matter how big or how small in value. 'Creativeness' means to put these principles into use. 'Completeness' means to commit oneself to the great path in life and to lack no virtue. 'Perfection' means to not be shaken or frustrated by external things.

"A developed person has attained these ten qualities, thus he has a great mind. The great mind embraces all things without leaving anything out. All things follow his mind. With sufficient support of all things, high freedom is achieved. Therefore, such a one can at the same time be any one thing and also infinite.

"Such a mind is like gold in a big mountain or pearls in deep water. Such a person does not struggle for wealth or profit. He makes no pursuit of nobility. He does not yearn for long life. He does not seek the thrills of fast living. He is not excited by glory. He is not worried by any distress. He does not consider himself glorified if the entire world is put at his feet. To be glorified is often to be unable to maintain the wholeness of a virtue. A developed one unites himself with the wholeness of the universe and knows no death."

Lao Tzu said, "Tao is serene and still, pure and unmixed. Metal and stone will make a sound if someone or something hits them. This shows the responsiveness of Tao. Concerning the existence of things, no one can decide what is right or wrong. The highly developed one follows nature and is naturally responsive. He feels disgrace when he responds to things with only the knowledge of the thing but not the law. He stands at the beginning of all things. His wisdom can communicate with spirits. Thus his virtue is broad and all-inclusive. His mind is intuitive and orderly, and both mind and spirit are responsive to the external world.

"Without participating in the path of subtle integration, no life being can be born into a form. A life cannot be enlightened unless it conforms to goodness and virtue. A person of full development maintains the form of their life being, thoroughly understands the principle of life, follows the great virtue and clearly understands the principles of nature. Great is such a one. Suddenly he appears, and suddenly he goes; all things obey him. This is the person of full development.

"The developed one unites himself with the path of subtle integration. Look for the path, it has no form. Listen to it, it has no sound. Still there is subtle existence in the midst of formlessness. There is a responding consonance in the midst of the soundlessness. Therefore, from the subtlest state it can give birth to all things. From the most sublime, it emits the subtle light. Though it appears non-existent and empty, it can supply the needs of all things. Its response is timely and relevant to all things, no matter how large or how small, long or short, far or near."

The True Ruler

Nineteen years after the Yellow Emperor was enthroned, he had earned support and obedience everywhere he ruled. He heard that Kang Cheng Tzu lived on Kun Tung Mountain, so he went to see him and asked, "I heard that you have reached the ultimate level of integral truth. May I request to know the most powerful energy of the ultimate level? I wish to use it to help the growth of crops to feed my people. I also wish to learn to control *yin* and *yang* in order to harmonize all things. How can I achieve this?"

Kang Cheng Tzu answered, "What you ask lies within the coarse material sphere of things, and what you want is to extend your influence over all things. Do you want to use all those unusual natural phenomena as opportunities to rule the world? Keeping to the narrowness of your mind, how can you understand the path of ultimate truth?"

Therefore, the Yellow Emperor separated himself from the affairs of state. He stayed in a specially built house with couch grass on the floor for three months. Then he went to make another request.

Kang Cheng Tzu was resting on his bed, facing south, and the Yellow Emperor approached him, walking on his knees. He bowed low, touching his head to the ground and asked, "I hear that you have reached the highest state of the ultimate truth. I beg to know how to cultivate myself to achieve eternal life."

Surprised, Kang Cheng Tzu sat up and said, "Well asked! Listen, and I will tell you the highest state of the ultimate truth. The high power of the ultimate truth is profound, subtle and unthinkable. It is too subtle to be seen. Do not bother to look for a way to see or hear it, but concentrate on your own pure undisturbed spirit, with your body upright. Your spirit must be quiet and your mind must be clean and pure. Maintain your body undisturbed, your spirit unshaken. By the practice of the Way you shall attain the goal of becoming eternal.

"Do not use your eyes to watch external things. Do not use your ears to listen to external things. No thinking should be undertaken by your mind. In this way your spirits will subtly embrace each other and your body will become enduring.

"Do not shake your mind and will. Do not let any external thing influence your mind. Thus your virtue becomes whole. To abuse your mind is the root of disaster.

"I shall help you go into vast space, reaching for the realm of high *yang* energy. I shall also help you return to the most profound realm of high *yin* energy. These two govern all heavenly bodies and the five elementary phases of natural energy. All things derive their lives from them. *Yin* and *yang* remain as their treasure.

"Pay attention to cultivating yourself. All things will naturally grow stronger and stronger. There is no need for you to manage them.

"I only concentrate on my single-purposed state of harmony, balance and calmness. Thus I have lived 1,200 years and my body shows no signs of decline."

The Yellow Emperor bowed deeply again and said, "Kang Cheng Tzu has become one with Heaven."

Kang Cheng Tzu said, "Listen to what I tell you. The changes of all things has no end, although worldly people may think there is a beginning and an end. The changes of things are not predictable, though worldly people might think they are. He who receives my guidance can be an emperor or a king. He who loses my guidance is ignorant and only sees the light of the sun and moon while he is alive. He then becomes soil and dust after death. When things are thriving, they obtain their lives from the earth. After they are withered, they shall return to earth again, but I go on my journey of boundlessness, roaming in unlimited space. When I disappear from the human world I share the same light with the sun and the moon. I live as long as the universe. When I come, I retain no knowledge of the disturbing world in my mind. When I go on my journey, I also retain no memory of worldly life experience.

"All people think that one must be subject to life and death and thus they must die someday. I understand the principle of the oneness of life and thus I live forever."

The Way of Total Integration

The way of total integration can be respected and trusted. It does not do anything in particular. It has no particular form. It can be passed on, but it cannot be tangibly received. It can be attained, but it cannot be seen. It is rooted in and originates from itself. Before Heaven and Earth existed it already sustained itself and marked the beginning of time. It gives birth to subtle beings as the different functions of all spiritual beings. It also gives birth to Heaven and Earth. It cannot be considered high, though it is prior to the ultimate law of the alternative operations of *yin* and *yang* and the five *chi.* It cannot be considered deep, even though it is deeper than the six dimensions. It cannot be considered old, though it has been growing since the most remote and ancient times.

Ancient people developed themselves through total integration. Shi Wei united himself with Heaven and Earth after finding the way of total integration.

Fu Shi entered the origin of primal energy after finding the way of total integration.

The Big Dipper attained the way of total integration, and makes no mistakes in leading the order of all Heavenly bodies.

The Sun and Moon attained the way of total integration and became long enduring.

Kan Pei attained the way of total integration and became god of Kun Lun Mountain.

Fun Yi attained the way of total integration to have the freedom of all waters.

Jan Wu attained the way of total integration and became god of Tai Mountain.

The Yellow Emperor attained the way of total integration and ascended to Heaven.

Chun Shu attained the way of total integration to become the divine sovereign of the North.

Yu Chuan attained the way of total integration to become the water god.

The Goddess of the West attained the way of total integration to become immortal on Shao Huan Mountain. No one knows when she begins or when she ends.

Pan Chu attained the way of total integration to live a goodly sum of eight hundred years from the time of Emperor Shun (2257-2208 B.C.) until almost the time of the Chou Dynasty (1122-265 B.C.) through the reign of all five strong princes.

Fu Shou attained the way of total integration to help the capable premier Wu Ding, Emperor of the Shang Dynasty (1766-1123 B.C.), and brought forth a peaceful world to rank himself as one of the bright stars among the twenty-eight constellations.

The Power of Spiritual Integrity

The feudal Lord of the State of Lu where Confucius was born (Shan Tung province) once said to Confucius, who had been appointed prime minister, "There was an ordinary person from the state of Wei called Ai Tai Tou who was very ugly, but people who have been with him all liked to be around him and did not want to leave his company. Women who once knew him would beg their parents to let them become his concubine rather than the wife of some other

man.   He never gave orders or initiated anything, but
responded harmoniously to what was right around him. He
did not have the position of a lord with the power to
influence people's lives, and he had no provisions to offer
people's bellies. As a matter of fact, he would scare people
with his looks, but he remained just what he was. He was
not widely known, but the men and women who knew him
were loyal to him. He possessed something different than
ordinary people. Therefore, I summoned him for my own
observation, and of course I found him physically unattrac-
tive, but my impression totally changed after being with him
for a month. I could appreciate what sort of person he was.
In less than a year I had confidence in him. At that time it
happened that the post of prime minister became vacant
and I decided to turn the office over to him. He did not
express great happiness in accepting, which embarrassed
me. Then right after I gave him the reins of government, he
quit and left. I was left with a feeling of great loss, which
made me realize that there was no one with whom I could
make my state happy. What sort of man was he?"

Confucius replied, "Once I was on a mission to the State
of Chu (Wu Pei province) and I happened to see some piglets
nursing at their dead mother. Soon they no longer saw their
likeness in her and they all left. It was simply because what
they loved in the mother was not her looks but that which
animated her body. So it is with the soldier who has died in
battle and is buried. He no longer needs the shield from the
side of his chariot. To those who lose their feet, shoes are
of no importance. In all these cases, it is the primary
condition which is gone.

"In the royal house, the fingernails of the maids are not
cut, nor are their ears pierced. Married servants are no
longer sent on dangerous missions. Even these lowly
servants are valued, so I think people of whole virtue need
to be valued even more.

"Look at Ai Tai Tou. He said nothing special and did
nothing in particular to earn people's love and trust, and yet
people were ready to turn their state over to him and were
only afraid that he would not accept. It must be that his

spiritual integrity is whole. His virtue takes no particular
form, but is naturally fulfilled."

"What do you mean when you say the power of spiritual
integrity?" asked Lord Au.

Confucius said, "To one who attained Tao, the Integral
Truth has said, survival, loss of life, failure, prosperity,
poverty, riches, worthiness, unworthiness, slander, fame,
hunger and thirst, hot and cold are merely the changes of
external life. They are the eternal processes of cycles. They
replace one another around us day and night. They should
not be enough to destroy your innermost peace. They
should not be allowed to enter your spiritual center. You
must treat them harmoniously and give each its due. Do
not let one particular situation cause you to lose the joy of
life or step back from all the natural changes coming at you
day and night. You should have a fresh spirit toward all
things and accept all changes as new opportunities. This is
called the attainment of 'wholeness.'"

Lord Au asked, "What do you mean that virtue has no
form?"

Confucius answered, "Virtue can be exemplified by water
that is quiet and centered without splashing around. Virtue
is what helps one reach peace. It has form because it is
whole, but since there is no special projection, there is no
form."

Nobility Resides in One's Spiritual Essence

Shen Tu, a man of low background, was a fellow student
of Tzu Chan, a man of high position. Tzu Chan said to Shen
Tu, "When I leave a place first, you should stay behind." On
the following day, when they were seated together, Tzu Chan
said to Shen Tu, "When I leave today, will you remain
behind, or haven't you made up your mind to show me
respect? When you see a person of position like me, you do
not even get out of the way. Do you think you are as
important as me?"

Shen Tu said, "Within the house of a true Master is there
any such thing as a special person? You put so much value
on your own authority that you would place others behind
yourself. I have heard that if one has a mirror and uses it,

one is able to keep the dirt off one's face. Likewise, he who stays with a virtuous one can remain free from bad conduct. You have been with the Master for a long time, and yet you talk like this. It's not right, is it?

"You, a man of no achievement, think you have reached the virtue of Niao! Look again. As I see it, there are lots of people who excuse their own mistakes and claim they do not deserve the consequences.

"In the sphere of human life there are things you cannot do anything about. To know this and be content with what you can attain is the mark of a man of virtue. All of us in the arena of life are playing in front of the excellent archer Yu. We are all in direct line of his arrows. Some are not hit, but that is just a matter of luck, not the result of the wisdom of the sages.

"There are lots of people who might laugh at the shortness of other people. They laugh at me and it makes me boil with rage. However, after I come here to the Master's place I feel calmer, and then I go home. I do not know whether he washes me with kindness, or whether I just come to understand things and myself. I have followed him for nineteen years and he has never once let on that he's aware that I'm inferior.

"Now you and I are supposed to be students of unlimited spirit. Yet you still use the physical level and external standards to judge things."

Tzu Chan immediately saw his error and said, "Please make no mention of the matter any more." He admitted his mistake.

The Infinite
At the time of the autumn floods, the hundred running streams pour into the Yellow River. So great is the breadth of the raging current that, looking from bank to bank, island to island, one cannot distinguish a horse from a cow. This made the Lord of the Yellow River full of joy, believing that the grandness of the universe was gathered within him.

With great rejoicing he followed the current east until at last he reached the North Sea where he could see no end to the water. Then he refocused his gaze and saw the Lord of the North Sea, and he sighed and said, "As the saying goes, 'One thinks he is better than everyone else when he first learns something about the Integral Truth. However, he neglects the fact that the Integral Truth is infinite.' This describes my limitation. I have also heard that someone belittled the intellectual achievement of Confucius and despised the virtuous practice of Po Yi, who yielded his throne to his younger brother. I could not accept what was said then, but now that I see the immeasurable vastness of the ocean I suddenly realize my own narrowness as I approach the gate of the Integral Truth."

The Lord of the North Sea replied, "One cannot discuss the ocean with a well frog, for he has been confined by the space in which he lives. One cannot talk about ice with a summer insect, for he is restricted to a single season. In the same way, you cannot discuss the Integral Truth with cramped intellectuals, for they are bound to their frag-mented education. Today you have gotten out beyond your shores and borders and have seen the great ocean. You have realized your own past shallowness and narrowness. Now it becomes possible to talk with you about the great Integral Truth of beingness and non-beingness.

"Of all the waters of the world, none is greater than the sea. Ten thousand streams flow into it. I have never heard of its depletion. It is not affected by the variation of the seasons. It is not bothered by flood or drought. Its capacity is much greater than any stream or river. I, the Lord of the North Sea, have never thought I am greater than any other waters, despite all that I can hold.

"I equate myself with all beings formed by Heaven and Earth, receiving energy from the two spheres of *yin* and *yang* and from the visible sources like the sun and the moon and all the stars. My being is like a tiny stone underneath a small plant on a huge mountain. I have just discovered my smallness; how can I take pride in my greatness?

"Furthermore, the four seas with all that is between Heaven and Earth, are they not like an anthill in a vast marsh? All of China, is it not like a grain of rice in a great storehouse? Among the number of things which can be named, mankind is only one of ten thousand. Though numerous people are gathered in the nine states of Chin where crops are grown and carts and boats transport people everywhere, the space that mankind occupies is only a small fraction of the earth. If you compare mankind to all things in the universe, we are like the tip of a hair compared to the whole body of a horse. And when you consider all of history, including the ancient emperors, the wars among the three kings, the sympathy of the great kind ones and the capability of all able people in all countries, this is still only a small range. If Po Yi thought he had fulfilled the high virtue of yielding, and if Confucius thought he was knowledgeably achieved, by priding themselves in this way were they not like you in priding yourself over the possession of water?"

The Lord of the Yellow River replied, "Well then, if I keep to the distinction between what is big as the highness of Heaven and Earth, and what is small as the smallness of the tip of a hair, is it correct enough?"

"No," said the Lord of the North Sea. "There is no single way to decide the right size for all different things. There is no end to time. There is no constancy in a single person's life. And there is no fixed point to decide the beginning and the end. Therefore, the integral mind views both far and near, recognizes the small without considering it paltry and recognizes the large without considering it colossal, for it knows there is no standard to decide the relative size of all things.

"The integral mind has a clear understanding of the non-separation of past and present, and for that reason the remoteness of the past does not evoke longing, nor does the brevity of the present produce anxiety. It knows that time has no end. The integral mind perceives the nature of fullness and emptiness and does not delight in acquiring something, nor does it grieve over loss, for it knows that no condition is permanent. Understanding that life and death are the natural path of life, the integral mind is not fixated on survival, nor does it look on death as a calamity, for it knows that there is no point that can be assigned to the beginning and end of life.

"In calculating what a man knows, it is always less than what a man does not know. In calculating the time a man lives, it is much shorter than the time which he does not live physically. With what is minimum, a man attempts to exhaust what is maximum. Therefore he becomes lost in great confusion. From this point of view, how can one decide whether the tip of a hair is the smallest entity or Heaven and Earth are the largest?"

The Lord of the Yellow River said, "Today's people, viewing things from the most minute to the largest, have reached the point that the most essential has no form, and the largest form is unable to be held. How do you interpret this?"

The Lord of the North Sea answered, "The smallest and the largest can still be handled by the mind because they have form. However, the formless cannot be measured or put under control. It cannot be expressed in numbers. What can be sensed is the coarse level of matter, and what can be understood by the mind is the fineness of things. Yet what cannot be described with words or examined by the mind is beyond form and has nothing to do with coarseness or fineness, because it is essential.

"Therefore, the integral one, the person who embraces his essential integrity, does nothing to harm other people. He does not abuse favors. He is not moved by profit. He does not despise inferiors. He does not contend for wealth or goods. He is not versed in refined manners or pretense. He does not depend on others' help in accomplishing his work. He does not abuse his strength in maintaining his life. He does not devalue himself by temptation or corruption. His behavior differs from that of the mob, but he makes no show of difference with uniqueness and eccentricity. He is peaceful and stays behind the crowd, but does not despise those who run forward to flatter and fawn. Titles and positions of nobility do not attract him. Persecution and punishment do not humiliate him. He does not discriminate between those who think he is right and those who think he is wrong. He does not favor the small or the large. This is what I have heard.

"In summary, an ancient saying tells us, "The integral one wins no fame. The one of complete virtue wins no gain. The great person has no self. He reaches the highest fulfillment of virtue by doing nothing against the integral nature of universal life."

The Lord of the Yellow River said, "Tell me, how do we distinguish the high from the low, the large from the small, whether by the interior or the exterior of things?"

The Lord of the North Sea replied, "From the point of view of the Integral Truth, things have neither nobility nor meanness. From the point of view of things themselves, each regards itself as noble and other things as mean. From the point of view of differences, a thing can be considered big whenever it appears bigger than something else, or small whenever it appears smaller than something else. So everything in nature is both big and small. Look at a big thing; it is self-sufficient within itself. Look at a small thing; it is also complete in itself. Then we can say that Heaven and Earth are as small as tiny grains, and the tip of a hair is as big as a range of mountains. Where can the law of differences be established?

"From the point of view of function, whatever shape something possesses is considered to be its existence. Whatever does not possess a shape is considered non-existent. By knowing East, West can be known. They cannot be known without one another. The existence of things can be known by the non-existence of things. Then we can say that all things are existent, or all things are not existent. Thus we can understand the function of totality.

"From the point of view of preference, if people follow their own preference, they approve of things according to their preference. They disapprove of things if they are not according to their preference. For example, a high moral standard was what Emperor Niao (2357-2258 B.C.) valued, and a luxurious and lustful style of life was what the Emperor of Chieh (1818-1767 B.C.) was most interested in. Naturally, they regarded things differently. It can be seen from this how preference creates difference.

"Something more. In ancient times, Emperor Niao abdicated to Emperor Shun (2257-2208 B.C.). It was a beautiful and peaceful transition of rulership. Later, Kuai, the king of Yen, imitated their beautiful behavior and abdicated his throne to Chih, his premier, but the state was destroyed by the invasion of a strong neighbor. Tang (1766 B.C.) and Wu (1122 B.C.) earned support and were enthroned by engaging in revolution. Later, Prince Po followed a similar way but was unsupported and wiped out by the people. You see, the element of time changes the meaning of behavior, whether noble or mean, and there is no constant rule in human society.

"The huge chariot, Liang Li, can be used to batter down a city wall, but it is no help in blocking a little hole. This is to show the difference of use. The famous horses, Chi Chi and Hue Li could gallop a thousand li in a single day, but when it came to catching rats, they were not as good as a cat or a weasel. This shows the differences in skill. At night the owl can see mosquitoes, but if it goes forth in the daylight, no matter how wide it opens its eyes it cannot see a mound or a hill. This shows the differences in nature.

"Now do you say that you are going to make right your master and do away with wrong? Or make order your master and do away with disorder? If you do, then you have not understood the principle of Heaven and Earth and the truth of all things. This is like saying that you are going to make Heaven your Master and do away with Earth, or make *yin* your Master and do away with *yang*. Obviously, it is impossible. If people insist on such bias, they must be either undeveloped or deceitful.

"People came into power at different times and in different ways. If the way fits the time and mode of society, one is respected as a righteous person. If the way does not fit the time and social mode, then one is regarded as a usurper. Thus, let us be quiet. O, Lord of the Yellow River, how can you know the significance of being considered noble or mean, and the real definition of large or small?"

The Lord of the North Sea added, "Viewing things with the Integral Truth, there is no difference between nobility and meanness because these are reversible. To hold onto one's preference for what to take and what not to take is also against the integral truth. In the integral truth that which is called "much" and that which is called "less" are changeable. Do not hold a particular way to be your definite way; you will be departing far from the integral nature of the universe. Be benign, like a deity who loves all things without any partiality. Be broad, like an open space, setting no borders on anything and embracing all things. This is called being upright without any conditions. All things become one. The integral path of the universe has no beginning and no end, yet things live and die. Thus, do not pride yourself on what has been accomplished. The years and months do not stop, times and ages do not stay. All things grow, prosper, ripen and decay, and then begin again after every ending. This shows the universal law of all things and all human matters.

"Once things receive life, they start to run around at top speed. Nothing is unchanging, and no moment is not reforming. So there is no need to search for answers about how to conduct oneself. Things change without our needing to manage them. Is this not so?"

The Lord of the Yellow River asked, "Then why should we respect the Integral Way?"

The Lord of the North Sea answered, "He who knows the integral path must have reached the understanding of the law of all things. He who understands the law of all things must know how to harmonize himself with all circumstances. Thus, the one who knows how to harmonize himself with all circumstances will suffer no harm from them. The one of integral virtue cannot be burned by fire, nor drowned by water. The changes of hot or cold cannot make him sick. Birds and beasts cannot harm him. This is not to say he makes light of them. He carefully inspects the range of safety and danger and peacefully faces happy and unhappy situations. With prudence he decides what he should accept and what he should decline, thus there is nothing which can harm him. This is to say that essentially, the nature of Heaven is internal. The code of human behavior is external. Virtue is nature. One needs to know what is natural and what is human. To follow nature, take your stand in virtue. No matter whether you are going or coming, stretching or holding back, always return to the essence of your being as I have described here."

The Lord of the Yellow River said, "How can we know the difference between what is heavenly in nature and what is artificial?"

The Lord of the North Sea said, "Horses and oxen have four legs; that is natural. To bridle a horse's head, and pierce the nose of an ox is artificial. Therefore, as human beings we say, do not let what is artificial destroy what is natural. Do not support any cause that would harm your life, and do not sacrifice virtue for fame. To keep to these principles without losing them is called returning to the original truth of your being."

Note: all of the above the stories are adapted and elucidated from the teachings of Chuang Tzu, an important Master who lived during the time written characters were beautifully and abundantly used for the first time. The last story has been a favorite of many eminent Chinese scholars for generations.

How can you achieve such great power of life as Chuang Tzu? Direct understanding and transplanting into your spirit and mind is possible, but all the practices I give in this book and others are ways to attain and embrace the Infinite.

The Importance of Reading the *Tao Teh Ching*

People generally associate the origin of Taoist teaching with Lao Tzu, but in reality, the teaching of Tao did not originate with the *Tao Teh Ching*. Before Lao Tzu there were many sages who were already living examples of integral beings. In addition to the *Tao Teh Ching*, the *I Ching*, the Yellow Emperor's book and the *Nei Ching*, several other spiritual works were already in existence which reflected the deep insight of the ancient sages. However, it is true that the Tao Teh Ching has become the most popular classic of later times.

The *Tao Teh Ching* reflects a profound wisdom that has been used and accepted for generations. Its exalted integral truth is actually beyond words, but peace, serenity and inner harmony are the rewards for the one who receives its essence. A lifetime endeavor is opened to those who accept its teachings. If there were any single book which I would unhesitatingly adopt as my spiritual guideline for life, this would be it. It is an inexhaustible treasure. It can lead many individuals as well as a whole society, in the present or in the future, on the right path of life. It is not like the books of a spiritual tradition or religion which sell preconceptions and create prejudice between people, or influences them to become destructive, aggressive and hot-headed. It is also not like those books which make people less vital so that they cannot face the reality of worldly life. Rather, it guides all people to lead a healthy and harmonious life.

While not going into it too deeply, I feel it is important to introduce a few of the basic principles of the *Tao Teh Ching* to increase your understanding of its importance as a guide for your spiritual development. From these principles you will see that spiritual development is not new, but is an expression of timeless universal moral nature.

There are three general spheres of life covered in this book: the sphere of physical health cultivation which enables one to live through the diversity of life; the sphere of mental clarity and cultivation which enables one to transcend one's own emotions and worldly confusion; and the sphere of spiritual purity and cultivation which enables one to achieve a high state of integration and unite with the universal integral spiritual realm.

More specifically, the *Tao Teh Ching* emphasizes selfless leadership along with selfless public service. In Lao Tzu's time, people were already competing for leadership and striving to be in a position of authority over others. The *Tao Teh Ching* does not exalt this kind of leadership, but takes the examples of past great Emperors such as Fu Shi, Shen Nung, the Yellow Emperor, Niao, Shun, Yu and others. Lao Tzu says that anyone who takes on the troubles of a nation is the true king or leader of that nation. A truly selfless leader or Emperor is one who finds the way to solve the troubles of all his people. Natural leadership is not a privilege or personal enjoyment of power, but a personal service. For this reason the *Tao Teh Ching* advises one not to be competitive, especially for leadership. If, however, the chance or opportunity comes to you, you must morally and courageously take the responsibility and fulfill your personal duty and moral duty of the time. Once you fulfill the obligation, do not luxuriate in your success or seek recognition for your work. When the mission is accomplished, it is time to retire or retreat from prominence.

We can find good examples of that kind of leadership both before and after Lao Tzu in Chinese history. Before Lao Tzu, those people ruled the country, but after Lao Tzu they were mostly advisors to the leaders. This means that while they did not put themselves in a position of leadership, they nevertheless influenced the leaders from a more humble position.

Another thing we learn from Lao Tzu is that a person does not need to be outwardly and recognizably meritorious, holy or virtuous. One only needs to naturally follow their normal nature. A truly moral person, living a normal life, will be indistinguishable in their morality. Even though they may appear amoral, they are still moral. Why? Because they will be expressing the balance of nature. Therefore, it is unnecessary to emphasize or take on any formal or lofty ethics.

Lao Tzu also clearly points out the importance of non-violence. In everyday life, few people are killers or even people of violence, but many people are emotionally violent. Many people lose their tempers when things do not go their way. The loss of spiritual qualities such as patience and tolerance make people take a violent emotional path. This is the true root of evil. Evil does not necessarily have a deep evil nature. Most people become evil because of a pattern of emotional violence, and many people commit emotional violence toward themselves. That is why harmony, purity and quietness are taught in the *Tao Teh Ching*. These will eventually resolve or reform personal emotional violence.

The *Tao Teh Ching* also stresses the importance of the direction of personal cultivation. First we need to make our bodies healthy, flexible and strong, but not strong in the muscular sense. We value the unconquerable gentle strength. That is what we need to cultivate, not the type of violent force that is so common today. It also suggests keeping away from unreasonable ambition and competition.

More important, we also need to develop wisdom as our inner subtle light and should harmonize this light with whomsoever we come into contact. We must never make anyone feel inferior or unsafe around us, but instead make them feel supported. And finally, follow a natural way of life like the developed ones. That does not mean you need to live as a primitive person, but live in harmony with nature. A spiritually achieved one is not a special person of external distinction. He harmonizes with the natural environment and does not appear as a miracle performer or special being. He is one who embraces Oneness, that is, the spiritual essence. In one's personal cultivation, oneness is the simple essence of one's own life being. The thing of importance in one's cultivation is to embrace one's spiritual essence.

The essential principles of spiritual cultivation and other important guidelines are contained in Lao Tzu's *Tao Teh Ching.* If you wish to learn more from Lao Tzu, my translations of his works are available in *The Complete Works of Lao Tzu* and *The Esoteric Tao Teh Ching.*

Chapter 3

Work to Improve
the Quality of Your Mind

Enhance Your Spiritual Life by Working on Your Mind
*This guidance comes from highly achieved beings who
were the teachers of Kou Shuan, the great-uncle of Master
Kou Hong. This instruction is valuable to those who cultivate
the Universal Integral Way. Do not misunderstand what has
been said by some ancient achieved ones like Chuang Tzu
and others when they say to never use the mind to control
the mind; they are expressing their high level of achievement.
They have finished with inner and outer battles. Their minds
are no longer disturbed, thus there is no need to control them.
For most people, however, there is a definite need for the
high sphere of the mind to guide the low sphere, which
includes emotions, desires, etc. To not do so is to continue in
ignorance and delusion.*

If you wish to cultivate Tao, the first thing to learn is to
give up all unnecessary activities. Then you can enter
spiritual centeredness through silent cultivation. When
your mind is too active, you cannot have peace, and you do
not know how to respect your true spiritual nature which is
connected with the universal divine realm. Until all dis-
traction is stopped, your fragmented mind cannot be put
together again. Distractions come from the sense organs.
Surely we depend on our eyes and ears and such, but even
if something glorifies or enriches you, all these things finally
become a burden on the reality of your eternal life. Until all
external temptations and sensory attachments are completely eliminated, whatever moves through your heart or your
mind will be regarded as important. So, while many people
wish to cultivate their mystical power, they must first learn
to give up their troubles, burdens and childishness.

Meditation! At one time the word only meant to calmly
sit down. In meditation what one needs to watch is one's
own mind. If any emotion, motivation or thought arises to
stir the peace of the pure mind, it needs to be gently

dissolved. You must work devotedly toward becoming undisturbed within to reach deep calm. If you are able to eliminate all strong, disturbing motivations, then sometimes the mind will float and roam. This random thinking also needs to be weeded out. Gently and quietly do this in the daytime and at night, never changing the path or stopping the practice. Never let something else become the lord of your mind, your body, or your being. Day and night, gently practice. Do not cut the real mind off, only the disturbed mind. Stay with the mind that has nothing in it, but do not stay with the mind that is something you can be aware of. Let your mind guide you toward a condition of emptiness, holding nothing but pure energy, nothing that has already been transformed into images. Do not fix your mind on any doctrine or idea, thus true spiritual energy will always be with you and will be nurtured and grow.

For the novice, it is difficult to stop the mind for even one second. You stop one thought and another follows on its heels, thus a battle rages inside. During the struggle, sometimes your whole body will start to respond physically. You may start to shake or perspire. Do not worry about it. If you are serious, cultivate yourself for a long, long time. Follow this way and continue to meditate. Then slowly you will become more skillful. Gradually you will attain innermost clarity and purity which are the foundation of the mind's power.

After you think you are skillful, do not stop. Do not give up the effort to pacify your mind. If you stop midway, then the attainment of eternity will be nullified by your interruption. This is a thousand-lifetime enterprise; you cannot regard it as something temporary. Sitting is just the beginning. When you walk, when you stand, when you lie down, keep your mind always unwavering, but let your spirit be naturally active without obstruction or harm. Whether you use words or not, whether there is any event or not, your mind is no longer bothered. It feels like you have no mind at all. In this way you can put yourself in the calm mountains. You can be on a busy street or in a noisy crowd, and your mind will not be cut to pieces by any external disturbance.

Here are a few special guidelines you should follow in silent cultivation. Do not restrain the mind too urgently or you will become sick and crazy. If your mind becomes too inactive, loosen your discipline a little bit. How loose? You need to find the appropriate point. Always make an appropriate adjustment. The mind must always be under your control. Even if you let your mind be active, still follow the right channel and right discipline as you have always done. When you are in a noisy, crowded place, do not indulge in emotions such as hatred or disgust.

When you are in an eventful circumstance and your mind is not disturbed, this is called true peace, true calmness. Your mind is no longer controlled by circumstance, it is free. The free mind is a powerful mind. It is a useful mind. It is the key to reaching the mystical source. However, remember that this true peace is attained by your cultivation, it is not a free gift.

After achieving true peace, the mind can grow wise. To some people wisdom comes sooner in their cultivation, and to others it comes more slowly. It does not depend on you, so never look for wisdom anxiously, because hurriedness can hurt your spiritual flow. If your spiritual energy is obstructed, then no wisdom can grow. If you cultivate yourself, you are not particularly looking for wisdom, but wisdom shapes itself within you; this is called true wisdom.

Do not confuse true wisdom with relative wisdom. All words and deeds that are recognized as being wise are conditioned by circumstance. Relative wisdom is like a beautiful bonfire that needs good firewood to burn. If problems did not arise, there would be no wisdom with which to solve them. People usually admire wisdom as they enjoy a good bonfire; it is seen as a bright achievement. However, it is not the true goal of spiritual attainment.

Once you have true wisdom, do not use it to show off. Wise people often appear to be simpletons. In this way they can benefit more people through their ordinariness, peace and simplicity. These triple beauties can reach to boundless realms. Therefore, in your silent cultivation, if too many things are held in your mind, they will attract other strange things which become disturbances by association, and you will never experience the effectiveness of a calm mind. If your mind is kept in the right channel, then the spiritual essence can be reached and high beings and things can be seen in your peace and calmness. The significance of that is the energy has transformed. However, special signs in your cultivation are no cause for excitement. Make nothing special of anything that happens beyond your true, peaceful mind. Let no more obstructions put your true, calm mind beneath them so there is nothing to support obstructions in you. Only the true mind exists purely, independently, solely and uniquely. Decrease all past contaminations daily, and do not engage in new accumulations. When you reach a state of no bondage, you are like a bird which breaks out of its cage and obtains freedom. If you keep practicing this, you will naturally attain Tao.

Anyone who attains the subtle essence of universal life will experience seven signs, or stages. I shall describe them to you one by one for your knowledge.

The first stage is when the mind reaches peace and easily responds to the subtle as well as the ordinary level of life. It is then easy to discern what worldly things are heavy and disturbing to your true peace, and thus a possible cause of a downfall.

The second stage is when old physical problems clear up by themselves and you do not need to go to physicians. Your body and mind feel light and happy.

The third stage is when your vitality is regenerated and you return to a natural and healthy long life. You also start to follow the right way of living as guided by your growing wisdom.

The fourth stage occurs after you have achieved the foundation of the first three stages. You can live as you wish and not be subject to the lower spheres of influence. You can then connect with the spiritual realm.

The fifth stage comes when physical energy is refined to be higher, more essential energy. Through serious cultivation, the physical energy is transformed into *chi.*

The sixth stage comes after transforming the gross *chi* into more subtle *chi.* Then you go further to transform your *chi* to be more essential, to become a spiritual being.

Spiritual beings can be in the world and remain subtle or not, as they choose. They are unfathomable and unpredictable. They are true spirits.

The seventh stage is when the spirit is refined and unites with the Tao. Then the ultimate being is achieved. This is a true Divine One. His light will then always respond to enlighten the darkness.

These seven steps to becoming one with Tao, or to attaining complete fulfillment, are universal. Anyone who engages in self-cultivation without seeing any of these positive results will not achieve Tao.

The absoluteness and uniqueness of spiritual achievement is unconditional and inexpressible. The expressible level manifests as peace and non-dualistic unity and has the power to dissolve all things back into the great oneness. This original spirit of freshness, is always with you in this and every moment. This spiritual truth is beyond the intellect; it is all-embracing and has great power.

Tao, as the initial spirit or the spirit of youth, is untouched and cannot be bent to any personal will or ambition. It never fails and never declines. The initial spirit is always in progress and always developing. It constantly provides the possibility for an entirely new range of life experience. This is the essence of universal nature. It does not hold to any past images. It does not necessarily value the common sense sayings of refined ancient sages. It is a great path discovered by transformable minds. As a self-cultivation, it refreshes one's spirit, mind and body, and brings all elements into one harmonious piece. If any method assists in achieving this goal of transforming oneself into a real being, it is a true path.

Thus, in true spiritual practice, we do not venerate old sayings, nor do we chant or say rosaries, mantras, etc. We live in and embrace universal nature. Any teaching of non-attachment which comes from fear is not the teaching of Tao. The "I-have-not-been-born-yet" spirit of correct cultivation expresses wholeness of spirit while leading a full life. We do not value quiet sitting or living in seclusion out of fear of experiencing life. We embrace wholeness of mind and willingly experience all necessary pain and trouble without being defeated or becoming cruel. We find growth in adversity and recover quickly from any minor setbacks. This is why the Integral Way is called the Great Path of Life.

Emotional Independence and a Balanced Life

It is fundamental and beneficial to attain emotional independence. It does not mean that one avoids all emotional relationships, or that you must live absolutely alone. It means that whether you associate with others or not, you remain independent.

Spiritual independence is a life-long pursuit without guarantee of attaining enlightenment or the discovery of the ultimate truth. Anyone who achieves spiritual independence must first achieve emotional independence.

What is emotional independence? Everyone has grown up in a family, or some kind of social unit where they learned to imitate adults as their knowledge of life developed. There they learned emotional dependence on others. Positively speaking, there is nothing wrong with living as part of a team where you trust each other and have loyalty and faithfulness to each other. It is especially valuable when you have love and emotional caring for each other. A problem arises with a person's constant demand for attention and being overly spoiled emotionally. Such psychological demands make a person an emotional cripple who cannot be an emotionally independent person. Most people have some emotional dependence, but they abuse it by looking for excessive support and attention. This is just emotional greed which makes family life become an emotional battlefield. People are like hunters, all the time hungry, looking for prey as sacrifice for their greed, for something to fill their cavity.

When people are spoiled as children, they grow up acting spoiled and thinking that somewhere in the world there is a great mother or father, or great wife or husband, or great friend who will always care for them emotionally. I do not think any such great person exists, but people build up an idea in their psy-chological framework and are always looking for such a person in their contact with others. In many cases, people make others victims by trying to fit them into their psycho-logical and emotional frames. Those people are innocent. They are not related to anyone's years of built-up psychological and emotional problems, yet they are immediately and unconsciously targeted as emotional prey. How unfortunate.

People often impose their emotional dependency on pets. Some people value their cats, dogs and birds more than humans; they are so innocent, they easily become people's emotional victims. Sometimes they learn to manipulate their owners back! When people become dependent on pets, they become emotional cripples. Once their dog or cat is lost, the person's whole emotional strength is gone. This is why to be a spiritual person, you must first achieve emotional independence. That is to say, you do not emotionally rely on anything.

Children's toys and games are so important in their emotional lives because they never learned emotional independence. In adult life, sports, gambling, games like Mah Jong and other things become emotional substitutes. Dear friends, people can use almost anything for emotional support in the negative sense. There are bad examples of unhealthy emotional life everywhere, typically between boyfriend and girlfriend, husband and wife, brother and sister, etc. People always engage in emotional competition, each one wishing to rule over the other emotionally. Sometimes for a few unimportant words, a big battle is started. In general society, or in families, jealousy is a poisonous element. People use jealousy to poison and harm one another. Why? Because people do not want anyone to be better than themselves, and at the same time they wish to be better than others. It is all so unnecessary. It is best to just pay attention to your own growth.

Siblings love each other, but because of jealousy they hate each other too. Their love/hate conflicts make their growth twisted and cause them to suffer. This inner battle continues for a long time and can be seen among many brothers and sisters and other family members as well.

In human history, among people and nations, the most poisonous element is still jealousy. People often start wars because they do not want anyone to be better or have more than themselves. They do not know that people can just be better by themselves without needing to do harm to others. Many lives have been lost through jealousy in all the generations; this has no meaning. These bad habits started in ancient times and are deeply rooted. Looking at modern people, have they improved their personal emotional elements? I do not think so. In daily emotional life, both men and women indulge their pride and egomania in different ways. They even refuse to admit to a small mistake like something not well done. When pointed out by a close associate, they will defend themselves madly and will even attack others for the sake of emotional revenge. This reactive pattern of poisonous emotions and struggle is repeated daily, which wastes useful hours or even days.

Spiritual people, on the other hand, are not allowed to be emotionally dependent on anything, not even their spiritual practices. If they are attached to forms and rituals, it is just another substitute for the contact that other emotional dependence is built on. It is no better than anything else. A truly spiritual person, who step by step gives up emotional toys, gradually comes to high emotional and spiritual independence. This does not mean that such people do not do anything, but only that emotionally they do not rely on toys. They enjoy all kinds of religious customs but they are not emotionally attached to them. They can even value and respect them without frowning upon them.

In my own personal experience as a spiritual teacher, it is happiness to enjoy the talent and good qualities of people who come together to enjoy pure spirit. However, sometimes people do not always come to look for truth and improvement, but for emotional victims. Those people try to emotionally influence you and impose something on you and spoil the whole soup. This happens often to spiritual teachers. I would say that the most difficult problem among spiritual students is their emotional dependence, just the same as it is in the ordinary world. This is why I am selective in my choice of students.

Many ascetics become hermits and do not expose themselves to people too much. Why? People will just emotionally abuse them. There is no wisdom to exposing yourself to a group of people if they do not know how to behave themselves. Fundamentally, all of us, including spiritual teachers, are human beings. Why should anyone suffer from emotional disturbance caused by other people? It is unnecessary and immature. It is a great joy to be with people of maturity. It is also a great joy to be with people of purity and innocence. It is a tremendous personal sacrifice if you are with a person who tries to make an emotional victim out of you. Emotions are rarely intentional, but they usually make a person blind to the reality of the situation.

If you are an independent spiritual teacher and worker, you must beware not to be emotionally abused or victimized by people. If you allow this, then you may simply be exchanging emotional suffering for material support. Therefore, I always say that a spiritual teacher or worker needs to look for financial independence and self-sufficiency instead of support from their students. Yet do not think that once a teacher is self-supporting they have no emotional difficulties with their followers. It is not that way at all. As a teacher, try to keep yourself away from immature people, and let them find their own way without your interference. Do what you can for the world, but do not get involved with dependent people. Do not make yourself an object of people's emotional or psychological arrows. Many spiritual teachers who suffer from the troubled minds of their students come to talk and receive health support from me, so I have a broad picture of the scope of this common problem.

It is valuable for all spiritual people to commit themselves for three, ten or fifteen years to help the world. If you are really serious, you need to organize your life and not be involved with groups of loose emotional people. Instead, involve yourself with well-disciplined people.

For the correct experience of emotions, everyone should have the experience of being married and living in a family and grow through their emotional troubles. Only when one's emotional trouble is finished can they look for spiritual achievement. Otherwise, you will always be circling in emotional suffering.

Most spiritual teachers or spiritual people sit on the shore and watch the rough waves of the emotional ocean. Only the person who truly swims in the ocean can understand the matters of life and true growth. That is what is important. People who sit on the shore and talk about life have never really experienced it; they are not truly achieved. They usually protect themselves in an ashram or a monastery and never have true experiences of human problems. Thus they do not really know how to help worldly people. By the way, a monastery can also be an ocean of rough waves too!

Eventually, no one can sit on the shore and watch people struggling emotionally in the water. However, if you are interested in self-cultivation, you will find that simplifying your emotional life is an important practice. Do not expend yourself emotionally too much. Everyone has emotions, but spiritual love is most valued. The point is whether you exercise your emotions positively or negatively. This is what distinguishes growth from degeneration.

Natural Celibacy

In the teaching of the Integral Way, the harmonization of two complementary elements in the *yin/yang* system is frequently used to explain all existence. This philosophy sometimes gives people the impression that the teaching of the Integral Way especially values sexual practices. This is not so. Sexual practice is only one small aspect of the Integral Way. Even though sex was neglected by many great religions of the ancient world, it has always been recognized as a legitimate part of spiritual cultivation. Yet, to discuss sex without mentioning celibacy is to tell only half of the story, so here I will focus on the value of celibacy.

Dear friends, sexual habits are different among all cultures, but celibacy has a real importance in human life

that transcends culture. It is helpful for a man before he is
twenty to restrain himself for purposes of health. If the root
of a young tree or young life is disturbed, the growing life
cannot become firm and may finish sooner. For a girl before
seventeen, chastity is valuable. It can be understood that
it is part of the personal value of being a woman. If modern
women can understand this point, I think that they will also
know the value of not being sexually permissive at any age.
People with the purpose of spiritual achievement in
particular need to observe celibacy before they are thirty
years old, and transfer strong impulsiveness to the pursuit
of wisdom, enlightenment and spiritual achievement.
During their thirties, when the *yin* or *yang* energy is at its
strongest, people of both sexes can correctly fulfill their
sexual desires. If you have a spiritual purpose, keep your
life simple, almost to the level of severity, austerity or
asceticism. Otherwise, looseness of mind, emotions and life
prevents what one wishes to attain. Eventually you hold
yourself at the same level without any achievement.

If a normal person in good health and in their thirties
is not timely paired, it will result in abnormal attitudes.
These abnormal attitudes can lead the person to mental
difficulties or criminal behavior. People without a spiritual
practice, or without the interest to be ascetic, must take
care not to go over the rim of their emotions and take
extreme actions. In the history of spiritual development,
many thousands of years ago, people thoroughly understood
the value of harmonization in sexual life, thus they never
over-emphasized the practice of celibacy. However, they
valued celibacy for purposes of health, spiritual achievement
or certain specific endeavors or cultivation. If celibacy is
done without a purpose, then one cannot have a clear mind
and will not be happy with a celibate life.

All spiritual life is flexible. Generally speaking, most
people wish to be paired, but not everyone finds their soul
mate or the best match. In this situation, the person needs
to be patient until a harmonious relationship happens. If a
relationship is chosen by the intellectual mind only, it will
not work well. If it is not the best choice for the person, the
result will be unhappiness. Some wise people prefer a

shorter arrangement and agree to stay together for a certain period. This is not always a bad idea.

If there is an opportunity to practice sexual cultivation, the average spiritual practitioner can certainly consider it. If a person is without such good fortune (as it is generally termed), and the best choice or match has not happened, and the second choice hasn't either, I recommend that you have patience and concentrate more on spiritual cultivation, because all opportunities in life offer you the possibility of spiritual advancement.

Sexual relationships are strongly emphasized in this society, which creates a psychological need for the opposite sex that can become a deep pattern in your emotional life. If you follow this way, you will either be disappointed and dismayed most of your life or you will eventually exhaust yourself. Therefore, all important spiritual practices begin with stopping the search for being paired; only do it if it happens naturally. There is a saying that expresses this principle, "Have the patience of a wise fisherman." It means that one does not pursue opportunity, but lets opportunity come naturally. A person can be receptive to the opportunity, but he or she should not have any expectations. Also, your decision to practice celibacy should not be the result of your environment forcing you into a certain way of life.

Many religious orders emphasize celibacy, and in some of those orders there is homosexual activity between members. This is wrong. If the choice of celibacy is due to spiritual pressures and goes against true personal needs, people become unnatural. Surely they value what they follow, but they make it meaningless.

Some people make an emotional commitment to celibacy when they are young. They try to fulfill this spiritual promise, but it is not a one-day or one-hour commitment. Life has different stages. The mind might decide something during one particular season of life when one's energy is astringent or shrinking. I recommend taking responsibility only for the moment you make the vow. No one can vouch for the next day, or next month or next year because change and growth are inevitable. A vow has no foundation when it is made forever. It does not mean that you are irresponsible for what you vow, it just means you have no knowledge of the next moment. If you become abnormal, it is because the practice of celibacy does not contribute to your health and is harmful to your spirit. Maybe you think that the tension built by an unnatural way of life can be released in some abnormal way. Why not just live normally in the first place? This is what I recommend for spiritual people. What is fundamentally wrong is the choice to be abnormal. It is not the broad human way. If your goal is to reach the supernatural, you first have to understand what is natural. If you go against nature, you can never reach the supernatural.

Most strict religious societies are suitable for only a few people, not the majority. Most people superficially follow such paths, but in their private lives they find they did not fully understand the situation. You cannot make a mature decision if you are at an immature stage of life. Celibacy must be a personal choice, it cannot be made by any external imposition. It must be the result of personal maturity and of understanding its value in supporting your health, your special research or your spiritual cultivation. Celibacy does have value, but it is not a doctrine. In and of itself, it is not the truth. For certain people with a special purpose, or at a certain stage of life when you are either too young or too old, or your health is not good, or you have a special assignment like soldiers on the battlefield, nothing but celibacy can make you strong physically, emotionally and spiritually.

For my friends who have a spiritual mission in the world, to women over forty, to men over sixty, slow down or directly adopt the principle of celibacy so that you do not keep wandering in the general field of paired life. This is also a good way to be happy. Do not think that only a married or paired life can make you happy. Pure celibacy can also make you happy, if combined with spiritual learning and practice. I have witnessed this for many years.

Spiritual beings who travel everywhere all the time, or those who stay in the mountains or rural places, do not look for a mate or reach out for communication with people.

They are special examples, but they do exist. They have achieved their life goal. I do not think everyone needs to follow their example, but they are good models for those who value personal freedom in life above anything else. Those beings enjoy closeness to nature instead of human relationships. I think their lives can help us understand emotional independence and the possibility of finding true happiness in that way for ourselves.

The practice of sex or celibacy depends on one's life circumstance; both ways have value. People who are paired or looking for a mate should not disrespect those who practice celibacy. I do not think those who practice celibacy will have any conflict with those who enjoy family life. If you are to fully enjoy or exercise the value of something, then some difficulty must be overcome, or some price needs to be paid. This is the world, this is human life, practically speaking. Family life provides a source of manpower, and the harness of that choice is no lighter than that of celibacy.

The Integral Realm
Q: How can we attain spiritual transcendence?

Master Ni: When I was a boy, I read widely and probed the vast world of modern civilization. I faced the drastic changes brought about by modern dualistic and fragmentary knowledge, and exposed my mind to the conceptual confusion of the time. Fortunately, the cultivation of the Integral Way helped me break through the obstacles to spiritual unity.

All the while, I used and appreciated a short invocation which my spiritual ancestors passed down to me. Any time I used it, it always put me back together again. People cannot escape today's flood of intellectual stimulation, but with this invocation, you can be like a boatman using a bamboo pole to help push your boat steadily upstream through the adverse currents. The following is that invocation. You may need to use it often!

Invocation of Total Integration

*The Integral Way has no form.
It cannot be obtained,
    it cannot be evaluated.
It can never be revealed or made extinct.
It does not come to you,
    nor does it depart from you.
There is neither a knower of it,
    nor a seer of it.
No one created it.
It is unspeakable,
    for no such thing as wisdom
    of self-delivery from the diversity
    of life can be mentioned.
Neither is there any realm
    after the attainment of such a way.*

*The Way is neither provable,
    nor disprovable.
This is not ambiguous speech;
    its non-dualistic nature is self-evident.
In following the Way,
    there is no reason to discriminate
    among things.
The Way is not alienated from the worldly way.
Neither does it differentiate between the ways
    which exist before and after it is reached.*

*Why is this so?
Because the Way cannot be thought of
    in the sense of being reachable or unreachable.
It is not separate from any ordinary
    moment of life.
There is no verification upon reaching it.
It is neither imaginable nor unimaginable.
It is neither doing nor non-doing.
The absolute truth is just so.*

*The Integral Truth behind all narrative ways
    of teaching is indescribable.*

One's attachment to specific learning
and beliefs at the narrative level
cause one to fail to reach
the suchness of the absolute truth.
The Way reaches the absolute
and bears neither a nameplate
nor has a distinct territory.
It cannot be expressed with thoughts.
It has no place to go and nowhere to stay.
It is against nothing.

The Way has no blessings to pursue.
It is neither obscure nor distinct.
Therefore, the Way has no boundaries
or limitations.
It is called the Path of Subtle Integration.
It could also be considered
the guidepost of self-cultivation.

Yet, for the Integral One,
there is no place where it is either needed
or not needed for cultivation.
All shall come to the great Oneness.
A more descriptive name for this
is the realm of no-action.
Why?
Because there is nothing to think about
or to fabricate.

Everything has its own nature,
yet all things are integrated
with the one Great Nature.

I would also give you a warning.
The Way is enlightenment to the ready mind.
But the Way may be poisonous
to a poisoned mind.
For people who have not reached the Way,
it is dangerous to pretend to be there.
It does poison you.

It takes your life and kills your soul
  with the snap of a finger.
Heed my warning when you decide
  to take the gift.

People of self-delivery,
  if inspired,
    try to discover the profound secret
    of being absolute,
    which is where true freedom lies.
An absolute being can light up the meaning
  of all worded and wordless teachings
  of all the ancient great minds
  in one instant.
He shall breathe the breath of all enlightened ones.
He dissolves his mind in the ocean of wisdom.
He shall reside in all the enlightened realms.

Chapter 4

Work to Be
in the Channel of Eternal Life

Observances for Self-Inspection
At the beginning of a spiritual pathway there can be no real progress made until one has purified one's energy. To think that anyone can begin with high level esoteric practices is to fool oneself. Many people have the contamination of many lives obstructing them, so the first thing they must do is cleanse and purify themselves. I know of no better way for beginning students to undertake this long and necessary step than by familiarizing themselves with these observances and then to put them into practice in their lives.

These observances are taken from two treatises that have been handed down for thousands of years: the *T'ai Shan Kan Yin Pien*, which I have called "Straighten Your Way," and the *Yin Chia Wen* or "The Silent Way of Blessing." They are discussed in more detail in *The Key to Good Fortune Is Spiritual Improvement*. The following excerpts will give you an idea of the principles underlying the observances.

Shan Kan Yin Pien: Straighten Your Way
The Divine One said, "Calamities and blessings do not come through any definite, distinguishable door; it is the person who invites them."

The rewards of good and evil are like a shadow accompanying one's body. The subtle response of the universal energy to one's mind and behavior is usually not recognized. Yet the accuracy of retributive operation unmistakenly happens to people, as if a spiritual being were keeping a record of one's evil deeds and determining the punishment by the seriousness of the transgressions. In fact, the quality and quantity of a person's life will truly be affected or drastically changed by how he or she thinks and behaves. When the normal standard of life is destroyed, one's health becomes poor and one's spirit becomes wasted. One often meets with sorrow and misery, and most people dislike such a person. Punishments and calamities in all forms pursue this person; good luck and joy shun this person; evil energy rays do them harm, and when the opportunity of life is exhausted, the person dies. Furthermore, there are actually spiritual beings who roam above people's heads and quietly watch them. People bear the marks of crimes and sins on their auras. Thus, they receive reprimands and retaliation from the different levels of the subtle realm. All enjoyment is stripped away; the enjoyment turns out to be poison. There are also evil spirits who come to reside inside the person's body to encourage the growth of evil. Those who seek everlasting life must first avoid all evil things.

Go forward if your deeds follow the Way; but withdraw immediately if they violate the Way. One who is good is respected by all. The Way of Heaven helps those who are good; happiness and wealth will follow them, all evil things will shun them, and spiritual beings will protect them. The person may even become a god.

It is traditional spiritual knowledge that one who seeks to become a divine immortal needs to fulfill 3,000 subtle, virtuous deeds. One who seeks to become happy and lead a long life on earth needs to perform 300 good deeds.

There are many who do evil deeds and later repent of their own accord and correct their behavior. By refraining from doing further evil and earnestly practicing much good, then in time good fortune will surely be obtained. This is what is called changing calamities into blessings.

Therefore, the person of good fortune speaks good, sees good and does good. If every day, one does these three kinds of good, after three years blessings will be invited and Heaven will come to help. The person of evil fortune speaks evil, sees evil and does evil. Every day, if one has these three kinds of evil, after three years one's evil being invites calamities and Heaven departs from this person.

Does this not convey that truthful words may not be beautiful and beautiful words may not be truthful? This is not merely beautiful poetry or an essay on eloquence. Neither is it a graceful work of literature or ornamental knowledge. It is the plain truth of life.

Commentary

The responsiveness of one's mind and behavior play a decisive role in one's personal fortune. A person's natural energy formation is fundamental to one's fortune. For example, a duck has a long neck but short legs. This is its natural formation. One would not try to cut off the duck's neck or try to lengthen its legs and thus have a more "desirable" duck. As for an individual's or a family's fortune, there are always some things longer and some things shorter. Likewise, for an individual's character, there are always some things that are longer and some that are shorter. The responsibility for one's life rests solely with the individual; it cannot be placed on external connections such as family fortune or social conditions.

To accept the natural conditions of one's life as they are frees one from the burden of concepts such as retribution, sin or guilt. However, just as an individual cannot be judged by his or her family background, neither can a family be judged by any of its individual members.

The process of nature is to evolve and transform, especially with regard to human life. The growth of an individual happens over the course of many lifetimes through varied life experiences. This is actually the meaning of evolution. Because we are constantly learning and growing, in every moment we are forming or reforming ourselves. The environment responds to what and how we are forming. As we change, our environment also changes; as it changes, does the subtle reformation of the spiritual environment continue to suit us? Each individual is responsible for every moment of his or her being. Tension creates tension, and self-dissolution creates dissolution of the subtle environment. The former is called negative creativity, and the latter, positive creativity. In the phase of physical life, harmony or balance is the highest virtue. Personal destiny is just the shadow of one's mind, or the pattern of one's dreams.

The science of astrology can tell general tendencies of the physical details of a life, but there is no predestined fate. Many children are born at the same day and hour each year, but each individual is unique and is thus responsible for his or her personal achievement, especially spiritually.

Their choices and efforts are what tell the true story of their fortune. In the general world, fatalism exists as a psychological escape for those who are self-defeated, but at the spiritual level, fatalism does not exist. Men and women can always do and be better if they decide to, spiritually.

Therefore, spiritual education is higher than the moral education of the cultural sphere. Yet, in a general sense, the two cannot be divided. A spiritual person is naturally a moral person, but a moral person is not necessarily a highly spiritually achieved person. On the spiritual level, real morality rests on the attainment of high spiritual awareness. This is natural morality. Natural morality rebukes the imitation of morality. Imitation morality is a mockery, it is not real. If things are not real, how can they be natural?

The moral education that is given to the vast majority of people is not natural because it is intellectual, but its source is the natural truth, and thus it should be valued and encouraged. Most people are not at a level where naturalness is beneficial to them. Whatever is natural cannot be considered moral or immoral, so on a deep spiritual level everything can be considered amoral. Morality only exists in the sphere of *yin* and *yang*, the relative world of duality. It is completely transcended at the level of the absolute.

In the long run, one cannot escape the moral way. To a highly achieved spiritual person, being moral exists every moment, it cannot be evaded. The foundation of natural morality is not cultural or religious. A life lived in harmony with the universe and the true self leads one to divine immortality after many years of sincere cultivation. Spiritual integration is natural morality, and natural morality is spiritual integration.

We need to discard all cultural and religious fabrications in order to experience natural morality, which is the natural health of life. They are merely expressions of suppressed and unachievable desires that are limited by the time, race and spiritual status of their leaders. Even if we do not know anything about religious fabrication, we may still know the truth of life. However, we can never banish natural morality, for it expresses how we are shaped and formed as real beings in any time, in any space, and in any lifetime.

Yin Chia Wen: The Silent Way of Blessing
The following work was written by an achieved one named Chahng O during the Tang Dynasty (620-950 A.D.).
For seventeen generations I have incarnated as a man of superior position, and I have never oppressed anyone. I have saved people from misfortune; helped people in need; shown pity to orphans; and forgiven people for their mistakes. I have extensively practiced the subtle virtue of doing good deeds without requiring anything in return. In this way, I became attuned to the Heavenly Way. If you too can set your mind on things as I have, then Heaven will surely bestow blessings upon you.

Refrain from doing evil, but earnestly do good deeds. This is the highest doctrine of all good religions. Thus, there will never be any ill influences upon you and you will always be protected by good and auspicious spirits.

Depending on how you treat others, immediate reward will come to you, and later rewards will reach your posterity. A hundred blessings will come to you like a chariot pulled by rushing horses; a thousand fortunes will surround you like auspicious clouds gathering above. If you practice the following aids to self-inspection, all good things will come to you through the Silent Way of Blessing.

Aids to Self-Inspection
The practice of immortality is the cultivation and refinement of individual energy through the body, mind and spirit, not as three separate entities, but as the integrated expression of one whole to reach for continual development.

The following observances are aids to self-inspection, after which one can begin to work on self-regulation. This is the foundation of self-cultivation. It is not through external beliefs or concepts that one achieves spiritual integration, but through the living reality that "to do is to be, and to be is to do." Thus, one's thoughts, words and deeds all reflect the truth of one's being.

Thoughts, Attitudes, Emotions

Do not cling to dualistic thinking and the juggling of relative concepts.
Maintain an integrated perspective; duality leads only to pain and weakness.

Do not become attached to the external excitement of worldly life.
Remain unattached. Where there is one inch of attachment there is one inch of spiritual entrapment.

Do not be self-opinionated.
Be humble and flexible. Maintain reserve when expressing opinions. No idea is absolute, and everything changes.

Do not disrespect valuable teachings or good writings.
Cherish enlightening writings, for they help liberate you.

Do not create taboos for yourself.
Be open-minded and know that taboos are self-imposed limitations and all limitations obstruct spiritual evolution.

Do not be superstitious.
Use your natural reason to direct yourself.

Do not be bored, discontent, or incapable of enjoying things.
Approach people and situations with freshness and openness.

Do not disrespect anyone, whether young or old.
Remember that the true nature of everyone is divine.

Do not be self-important and have excessive pride.
Think of others first and yourself second.

Do not feel hatred toward others or yourself.
Look for and support the good qualities in others and in yourself.

Do not rejoice in the misfortune of others.
Regard the health and happiness of others as an achievement of your own life, and a reality of the well-being of the world.

Do not be needy and dependent.
Take responsibility for yourself, for only through independence will you develop strength and maturity.

Do not be competitive for glory and exceptional profit.
Be content with the simple blessings of a plain, good life.

Do not be too proud to seek advice when you are in a new place or new job.
Value cooperation with experienced ones in all circumstances.

Do not be fearful and apprehensive.
Always look at the objective facts.

Do not ignore your own virtue.
Remain faithful to what you know to be true, regardless of possible unfavorable consequences.

Do not be vain, conceited, or superior to others.
Be yourself and matter-of-fact in any circumstance.

Do not hold any prejudice.
See things as they are.

Do not be insensitive, inconsiderate or abusive toward others.
Help and support others in positive ways.

Do not be pessimistic and focus only on negativity.
Take things as they are without emotional exaggeration.

Do not be stubborn and unreasonable.
Be receptive to good advice and learn to yield.

Do not allow others to use or abuse you.
Always examine yourself and do not allow someone to use you for their evil motives.

Do not be fanatic.
Remember that anything in excess gives birth to its opposite.

Do not be easily impressed with power.
The world's power seekers can be overwhelmed by someone stronger; a virtuous one cannot.

Do not judge others.
Take others as good or bad examples to work on yourself.

Do not expect to be rewarded after doing someone a favor.
Always do good for its own sake.

Do not be dismayed that there are only a few good people in the world.
Set a good example by your own behavior.

Do not be jealous of other's accomplishments.
Give due admiration and improve your own work.

Do not be elated when you are honored, or depressed when you are disgraced.
Maintain equanimity in all situations without letting external circumstances cause any spiritual loss.

Do not be greedy, lustful or overly desirous.
Be moderate in your needs and be content once you reach your goal.

Do not be moody or fussy.
Maintain calmness and be considerate of others even if it means suppressing yourself at times.

Do not hold narrow, superficial views.
Keep cultivating yourself in order to broaden your vision.

Do not embrace unrighteousness, even if it is fashionable.
*Be a careful student of human history and observe the
eventful results of correct purpose and correct means.
Then hold firmly to righteousness.*

Do not be insincere.
*Remember the universal law of energy response.
Insincere behavior will find an insincere response.*

Do not jump to hasty conclusions.
*Roughness and rushing is for careless people of little
achievement. Evaluate things carefully while looking
at the whole picture.*

Do not be overly emotional.
*All people have emotions, but do not be overcome by
them as children are. Always quietly guide your energy
in the right channel without rushing over the rim.*

Do not envy the prosperous.
*Appreciate the virtues and spiritual development of
others rather than their material conditions. Be content
and thankful for what you have.*

Do not blame others.
Take responsibility for everything that happens to you.

Do not be hypocritical.
*Do what you say and only say what you know you can
live up to.*

Do not be critical of others.
You would do better to apply the criticism to yourself.

Words
Do not exaggerate or lie.
Always speak the truth, but avoid injuring others.

Do not make prophesies that would stir up problems.
*Be cautious of the effect your words have on the peace
of the world.*

Do not pray foolishly or selfishly.
Be self-responsible and maintain integrity. Excessive prayer can create an unnatural dependence.

Do not ridicule, slander or defame the reputation of others.
Give credit where credit is due.

Do not brag or boast about your own goodness, achievement, or talents.
Allow others to discover your virtues for themselves.

Do not gossip or spread rumors or continue a fabricated story.
Stop the story-telling when it reaches you.

Do not mislead others with "half-truths."
Be accurate and clear and complete in your communications, or do not say anything at all.

Do not teach evil.
Remember that evil will swallow the teacher too.

Do not reveal the shortcomings or secrets of others.
This is mostly for your own protection.

Do not talk incessantly.
Be silent unless asked to speak.

Do not be sarcastic or insulting.
Be gentle and respectful in all your conversations.

Do not manipulate people with flattery and then talk about them behind their back.
Compliment someone only when it is appropriate and sincere.

Do not always be complaining, especially about the weather or natural disasters.
Treat nature as nature.

Do not demand anything from anyone.
*Material or psychological demands increase your
burden.*

Do not argue.
*It is through understanding, not argument, that one
wins friends.*

Do not cast spells or curse others.
*Your words have power; to behave foolishly is to be
foolish.*

Do not make fun of or belittle others.
Encourage and uplift others in order to uplift yourself.

Do not be impolite or verbally abusive.
*An undisciplined tongue and unruly thoughts invite
trouble.*

Do not teach things you really do not know.
*Share yourself openly with others and teach only what
you know to be true from your own experience.*

Do not vent your frustrations on others.
*Maintain silence and resolve the conflicts within
yourself.*

Do not ask things of people unreasonably.
Keep your request only to what is necessary.

Do not engage in sophistry or speak in a pompous style
that would confuse others or make them feel inferior.
*Speak clearly and simply to the level of the person or
group you are with.*

Do not use obscene language.
Maintain purity in your speech.

Do not speak with a forked tongue or try to appear
straight when you are crooked.
*Be honest about yourself, even if it does not make you
look good.*

Do not scream, shout or speak in a loud manner.
Most things can be handled quietly.

Do not comment on other people's mannerisms.
*Be non-judgmental of others, whether it is their looks,
speech, customs, or attitudes unless they are your
students or your children.*

Do not complain about the food you eat.
Be thankful for the food you have.

Do not comment on another's teacher or elders.
Respect the choices of other people.

Deeds
Do not hurt or kill any life unless absolutely necessary.
*Nurture and encourage life. Destroy only what is
harmful to other lives.*

Do not take your own life.
*Only if the sacrifice of your life saves the lives of others
is it justified.*

Do not keep pets or livestock for eventful slaughter.
Be merciful to animals and let them be free.

Do not pick flowers, cut trees, set fires or otherwise
destroy the environment for no good reason.
*Learn conservation and live in harmony with nature
instead of disturbing it.*

Do not have an abortion except in rare circumstances
such as danger to the mother, rape, incest or deformity of
the fetus.
*Human life is a sacred and rare opportunity for spiritual
evolution; it should not be taken away for mere
personal convenience.*

Do not encourage other people to kill.
Encourage love, compassion and respect for all life.

Do not put birds or animals in cages, except fierce ones.
Allow creatures their freedom, just as you want your own.

Do not disturb hibernating animals if you live where there are any.
Be respectful of their natural life cycle, just as you would expect to not have your own sleep disturbed.

Do not steal eggs from birds in the wild.
Consider your position in the universe and the limits of your natural rights.

Do not watch people kill birds or animals.
Avoid even indirect participation in the harming of any creature.

Do not frequent or visit a bad place or remain in an unhealthy environment.
Be sensitive to the quality of energy where you live or work, and if it feels unnatural or unhealthy to you, try to change it or move to a better place.

Do not participate in lewd conduct or watch obscene things.
Your mind and heart should not be the gathering place of impurities.

Do not seduce the young or naive.
Develop yourself so that you can encourage growth and maturity in others.

Do not be untidy, dirty, or live in filth.
Maintain purity in your external environment, whether at home, work, school, or in your car.

Do not sleep with another person's man or woman.
Respect the relationship between two people and do not create any cause for conflict or complication.

Do not eat spices unless for medicinal purposes.
Try to appreciate the simple flavor of plain foods which are healthy, and do not destroy the sensitivity of the taste buds.

Do not commit incest.
Respect your familial role and assist your family's well-being.

Do not eat red meat or drink alcohol or other improper food and drink.
Study the nature of different foods to understand what is beneficial and what is harmful to your body, and why.

Do not expose your body or bathe nude in public.
Practice modesty in dress and behavior so that you do not purposely disturb the minds of others around you.

Do not flirt with people.
Maintain dignity and reserve in your relationship with people.

Do not tatoo your body.
Appreciate the natural beauty of your physical form and treat it with care and respect.

Do not watch the sexual intercourse of animals.
Avoid watching anything that would overstimulate you and respect the privacy of all beings.

Do not build a house on an old grave site.
Have respect for the dead and be conscientious of the kind of energy that exists around your dwelling.

Do not participate in funerals if it can be avoided.
Fulfill your relationships with people while they are living; there is only unbeneficial energy around a corpse.

Do not waste your time or energy.
Take advantage of the opportunity that life provides to refine yourself and develop your virtue.

Do not have loose or reckless contact with women (men).
Manage your sexual energy responsibility. If there is no love, there should be no sex.

Do not eat bad food or food from an unknown source.
Eat only pure, clear, light food prepared with good will.

Do not make love with someone who is recently widowed.
If you become involved with such people it is easy to incur the revenge of their dead spouse.

Do not organize people for violent purposes.
Bring people together for healthy, constructive and positive endeavors only.

Do not carry a weapon in a threatening manner.
Work to promote peace and safety among people.

Do not destroy the things of others.
Respect the property of others by treating it with the same care you would give your own.

Do not rob others.
Live by your own strength, otherwise someone stronger than you will draw from your holdings.

Do not incite a riot.
Achieve harmony within yourself and encourage it among others.

Do not endanger others to gain safety for yourself.
Learn for yourself the true value of life, and then apply this knowledge to all lives.

Do not victimize others.
Treat others well and be of service to them.

Do not use violence or assist the violent to get what you want.
Maintain peace in your environment and your interactions with others, and give up whatever you desire that cannot be attained peacefully.

Do not participate in treacherous collusion.
Be honest and fair in all interactions, whether for social or business purposes.

Do not use your superior talents to manipulate or cheat simple people.
Use abilities where they will best serve all people.

Do not spy on others or meddle in their affairs.
Respect the privacy of others.

Do not read other people's mail.
Be trustful of other people's activities.

Do not seek revenge when you are mistreated.
Forgiveness begets power and cooperation.

Do not neglect the elders of a family or group that you visit.
Treat them with due respect and you will easily attract their support.

Do not be rude to the elderly.
Be respectful and attentive to the elderly and willing to learn from their life experience.

Do not take credit for other people's work.
Accept credit only for what you have done and acknowledge any assistance you have received from others.

Do not be a burden to others.
Make yourself useful in whatever capacity you can.

Do not use black magic on others.
Use your natural knowledge and abilities to heal and serve others.

Do not abuse others or yourself.
Be loving and respectful of your own life and that of others.

Do not look for causes or issues in order to display your benevolence.
Offer your services to others impartially and wholeheartedly, and keep a low profile.

Do not associate with evil people.
Seek out the company of wise and virtuous people. It is better to be alone than to keep bad company.

Do not bewilder others so that they look inferior.
Be sincere in helping them if they are truly inferior.

Do not take advantage of people's weaknesses.
Strengthen your own virtue.

Be aware that your own or other people's weak personalities cannot be trusted.
Strengthen your own personality as the fundamental goal of spiritual cultivation.

Do not misrepresent yourself to swindle others.
Be honest and above-board in all your dealings.

Do not compromise your natural virtue for popularity.
Maintain your virtue even if it means social isolation.

Do not monopolize on your good position.
Use a high position to serve others more expansively.

Do not borrow anything without returning or repaying it.
Develop your independence, and if you do borrow something, be diligent about repaying it.

Do not make trouble for other people or obstruct them.
*Think of ways in which you can ease people's burdens
and help their lives go more smoothly.*

Do not be deceitful or devious in your actions.
Be straightforward and willing to cooperate with others.

Do not disgrace others.
Work to help others live virtuous, productive lives.

Do not keep slaves or too many personal attendants.
Encourage everyone to be free and independent.

Do not accept gifts without doing something in return.
Keep the tally even to not incur a sense of obligation.

Do not accept gifts just because you helped someone.
*Helping people should be a natural response and no
reward should be expected.*

Do not seek favors by scheming.
Be guileless in your social interaction.

Do not associate with people just because they are
socially important.
*Build your relationships on the basis of personal virtue
and mutual respect.*

Do not associate only with relatives.
*Broaden your sphere of activity and relationships
beyond that of your family so you can see that the
whole world is one family.*

Do not interfere with or separate people's families.
Encourage and promote harmony within all people.

Do not create artificial desires or misinform people
through clever advertising tactics.
*Work to inform people of what is true and virtuous, and
present the facts clearly and honestly.*

Do not support someone just because you are close to them.
Be fair minded and objective in all aspects of your life, especially who or what you support.

Do not abandon the elderly in their later years, or the young in their early years.
Care for and be merciful to the old and the young, and fulfill your responsibilities in life as those who raised you fulfilled theirs.

Do not stare at people or make faces at them.
Be considerate of the feelings and peace of mind of others and work to dissolve antagonism.

Do not collect money to carry out fashionable worldly projects.
Put your time and resources into helping individuals cultivate virtue.

Do not favor one child or student over another.
Practice unconditional love toward all.

Do not lower other people in order to raise yourself, or lower yourself to raise an improper person.
Follow your own natural path and progress in life, and allow others to do the same.

Do not frighten people or make them fear you or anything else.
Help others become strong and virtuous individuals with the courage to face different circumstances in life.

Do not hold a position of power in which you would bring harm to people.
Only do work that contributes to the well-being of others.

Do not keep the company of soldiers or hired mercenaries.
They may not be evil themselves, but such people have accumulated energy that may influence you negatively.

Do not try to bribe spirits in order to get special favors.
Spirits help the one of righteousness only.

Do not take bribes or instigate bribery.
Develop your virtue, not your pocketbook.

Do not be a middleman to any unethical or immoral business.
Engage only in business practices that are constructive and beneficial to people.

Do not endanger women and children.
Realize that people's natures are different according to their age and sex, and act accordingly without expecting everyone to be the same.

Do not take part in a conspiracy.
A righteous person does not become involved with conspiracy.

Do not hesitate to make an offering of help to a spiritual worker.
Support all sincere efforts to realize their spiritual goal.

Do not unreasonably abandon your friends.
Be loyal and trustworthy.

Do not gather people together without doing good.
Put your energy to use for worthwhile, constructive purposes only.

Do not be disrespectful of the customs of other countries or any new place.
Broaden your understanding and tolerance of human habits to include all manners and forms of behavior.

Do not run around with shallow, irrelevant people.
You are subtly influenced by the company you keep. Be conscientious in your choice of friends.

Do not offer help or service unless it is requested of you.
*Allow people to develop mentally, physically and
spiritually in their own way, at their own pace.*

Do not create any disturbance when you move or when
you stop moving.
Let your physical presence cause no fright to others.

Do not waste things.
*Use things to their fullest extent and wherever possible
replenish what you take from nature.*

Do not bury useful items in graves.
*Useful objects in the physical realm are made to be
used by the living to support life.*

Do not put spiritual objects or sacred writings in unclean
places.
*Treat such things with honor for they are a means to
your spiritual development.*

Do not store poisons.
*The storage of poison gives a negative influence to its
environment.*

Do not mistreat vehicles or other machines that are
useful.
*A useful inanimate object that is the product of the
creative human mind deserves respect and care.*

Do not waste water or cause floods.
*Without water we could not sustain life on this planet,
so use it sparingly and respectfully.*

Do not overindulge in anything.
Practice moderation in all matters.

Do not behave recklessly or irresponsibly.
*Practice discipline with diligence so that you can control
and restrain your behavior.*

Do not be lazy, slothful, or inert.
*Put your energy and enthusiasm to use in some creative
project that is natural and healthy and that contributes
to your well-being and that of others.*

Do not do shoddy work.
Be conscientious in all that you do.

Do not always be searching for excitement.
*Live simply and quietly; this frees the mind and
promotes well-being.*

Do not be miserly and hoard things when so many are
without.
Be generous in giving to the poor whenever possible.

Do not live in opulence.
Be content with what you have and put it to good use.

Do not desire or covet the goods of others.
*Cultivate self-contentment and respect virtuous
achievement.*

Do not wander about or travel aimlessly.
Channel your restless energy into constructive activities.

Do not reserve the best enjoyments for yourself.
*Let good fortune come to you naturally rather than
trying to manipulate things to your advantage.*

Do not search for rare things.
*The truest and rarest of things are found within
yourself.*

Do not practice devil worship.
*Seek the depths of spiritual truth, not superficial
worship of the spirit world which leads to even further
separation.*

Do not ignore a main principle and stubbornly follow what is of minor importance.
Examine yourself for fixed attitudes and be open to a deeper experience of life.

Do not do anything that must be hidden from parents or superiors.
Follow the instructions and understand the wishes of your parents and superiors.

Do not set a bad example in anything you do.
Be a source of inspiration for others in the way you conduct your life.

Do not respond if someone angrily calls your name.
Wait until the person is calm and balanced before interacting with them.

Do not make your spiritual teacher into a social ornament.
Look only for how you can best serve your teacher, not how he can serve you.

Do not be lazy in the cultivation of spiritual immortality.
Be diligent in nurturing your energy and maintain constancy in your practice.

Do not go against our good tradition.
Express the same attitude and great heart as the ancient masters.

Do not berate yourself if you fail to keep any of these observances.
Correct yourself immediately and learn from experience.

Read these aids to self-inspection aloud whenever you feel spiritually unsafe.
The reading itself will open you to all the good spirits who will come to help you.

Summary of Soul Purification

1. <u>Eye Purification:</u> Do not look at corpses. It hurts your *chi* and makes you morbid. Do not look at pornography or low-class dancing and shows. If you violate these prohibitions, it will be difficult to have peace of mind or bear good fruit in your cultivation.

2. <u>Mouth Purification:</u> Do not eat raw meat, stimulating spices, or drink stimulating drinks. Do not use profanity or speak harmful words. In general, if you do not speak too much you will be able to help nourish your *Shen Chi* which is the virtuous energy used to cultivate ourselves.

3. <u>Body Purification:</u> Keep yourself physically and mentally clean. Anyone with whom you have sexual intercourse must also be physically and mentally clean, because if you sleep with an impure person it will stain your own soul. Also, do not use stimulating or addictive drugs. Do not depend on tranquilizers of any kind.

4. <u>Nose Purification:</u> Avoid dirty, decayed and strong smelling odors, for this hurts your *chi*. In order to keep your soul's terrace (*Ling Tai*) pure and maintain your sensitivity, avoid inhaling drugs.

5. <u>Ear Purification:</u> Avoid noise, low-class music, and listening to excessive talking because it will disturb your mind and hurt your *chi*.

6. <u>Mental Purification:</u> Do not have unrighteous or excessive ambition. Too much ambition will stir up your mind, while good motives purify your mind. Calmness can unite your soul with the reality of the universe and can make you effective in the right way, thus helping you become a *Shien.*

Chapter 5

Work to Integrate Your Spiritual Essence

On the Road of Self-Cultivation

The Origin

Before Heaven and Earth come into being
and Tai Chi is not yet manifest,
there is only the Great Silence,
the source of life.
It has no form, no name, and is made of nothing,
and yet as the Eternal Breath of Tao
it contains all.
It is, in its creative subtle energy,
continuously manifesting.
We call it the Mysterious Mother.
In her divine embrace she nurtures all life.
We call it Tao, the Subtle Origin.
All life depends on it.

From the Eternal Breath of Tao came forth
spontaneity as universal law.
Movement and change,
Tai Chi revolving in time and space,
and the interacting yin and yang energies
form all manifestations in the relative sphere.
This is the fundamental principle of the universe.
This knowledge has been handed down to us
by our revered spiritual ancestors.

* * * * *

Tao is great in all things,
    complete in all,
    universal in all,
    whole in all.
These three aspects are distinct,
    but the reality is One.

The Law of Great Energy Transformation

All manifestations of life with its changing events
*   depend on the Heavenly order of energy transformation.*
The subtle workings of the universe
*   cannot be fully understood by the mind.*
But to help you in your self-cultivation,
*   our spiritual ancestors formed the subtle truth into*
*   words and images as a tool to reach the*
*   depth of true understanding.*
They handed down to us the esoteric knowledge
*   of Heavenly order.*

Energy Formation Manifested as Beings

In the center of the universe,
*   nourished by the divine energy of the Mysterious Mother,*
*   resides the Jade Emperor,*
*   the undecayed one, self-so,*
*   called "Ti" in ancient times.*
His energy is most supreme.
His light illuminates the universe.
Its brilliance is all-encompassing.
This is the core of all manifested life.
From this center, radiating out to its circumference,
*   from the most subtle gradually changing to coarse,*
*   all spiritual beings receive this light.*
All natural and supernatural deities, sovereigns
*   and spirits surround him.*
They are very subtle beings,
*   and the most subtle of all are the Shiens.*
Their energy is highly refined and pure.
They can be with or without form,
*   and have reached perfection and self-mastery of life.*
They have become immortal through continuous self-renewal.
*   They are, together with the living Master,*
*   our guides in self-cultivation.*
To evolve to this high and pure manifestation of being
*   is the goal of one who follows the Way of universal truth.*

Yin and Yang

From interaction within the Subtle Origin,
  the Mysterious Mother,
  all phenomena of life come forth
  through the balancing energies of yin and yang.
Yang energy, referred to as Heaven,
  is subtle and spiritual.
It is creative and active by nature.
Yin energy, referred to as Earth,
  is coarse and physical.
It is receptive and cooperative by nature.
Yin and yang support each other in perfect harmony.

The Five Elementary Phases of Energy Transformation

The five basic types of energy are symbolized by
  fire, metal, water, wood and earth.
They manifest the relationship between all
  universal energies.
They penetrate sub-energies
  and have their own main function.
Each phase of transformation has a
  positive and negative, a yang and a yin,
  and within each phase the five phases
  are contained.
They work in perfect order and embody harmony.
When the natural order is disturbed,
  disharmony results.

* * * * *

To give birth,
To nourish,
To give birth without taking possession,
To nourish without appropriation,
To be chief among men
      without managing them,
This is the Mystic Virtue.

The Law of Change

All universal laws are under the governing law of change.
In daily life the five phases of transformation
*   are present in every event.*
There are five kinds of relative situations
*   existing at the same time, and every change*
*   can manifest one of the phases.*
The law of relativity is illustrated
*   by the five basic types of energy.*
The Book of Changes is the tool
*   to fully understand this universal law.*
Under the Law of Great Transformation,
*   the energies are constantly changing,*
*   never static.*
Their movement in change is constant.
Therefore, the future of a person has several possibilities,
*   but nothing is certain until the person makes it so.*

* * * * *

Before Heaven and Earth existed,
        there was something nebulous.
Silent, isolated, standing alone,
        unchanging, eternally revolving,
        worthy to be the Mother of All Things.
I do not know its name,
        and address it as Tao.
If forced to give it a name,
        I shall call it Great.
Being great implies reaching
        out in space.
Reaching out in space
        implies far-reaching.
Far-reaching implies
        reversion to the origin.

The Three Realms of the Universe

To have some understanding
of the subtle workings of the universe,
we categorize the different energies as "realms."
There are three realms of existence.
The spiritual realm, referred to as "Heaven,"
or the Realm of Utmost Purity,
contains spiritual power.
The mental realm, referred to as "Man,"
or the Realm of Crystal Purity,
contains rational power.
The physical realm, referred to as "Earth,
or the Realm of Great Purity,
contains organic power.
Those realms also exist in the physical body.
The spiritual realm resides in the head.
The mental realm resides in the heart.
The physical realm resides below the navel.
These are the three Tan Tien.
Since a human being is a miniature universe,
all cosmic laws are the individual's laws.
Gathering the coarse and subtle in his form,
a person stands between Heaven and Earth.
The mind is the instrument to unite
the spirit with the physical body.

* * * * *

The limit of the unlimited is called fullness.
The limitlessness of the limited is called emptiness.
Tao is the source of both,
    but it is neither full nor empty.
Tao produces both renewal and decay,
    but is neither renewal nor decay.
It causes being and non-being
    but is neither being nor non-being.
Tao assembles and destroys,
    but is neither the Totality nor the Void.

Guidelines to Self-Cultivation:
Understanding Mind in Macrocosm and Microcosm

Behind all phenomena is a universal mind.
The origin of humankind is very subtle,
*   and is brought forth by this universal mind.*
Our mind, in this physical body, is also very subtle
*   and was formed in this universal mind-energy.*
Through the mind we manifest our function in life.
Depending on the use of your mental energy,
*   you weave the pattern of your life.*
Man has received his mind as an instrument
*   to unite the spirit with the physical body.*
He has the ability to move his mind in the
*   direction of his choice.*
He can follow his instincts and desires
*   and move downward into the more physical realms,*
*   or bend his desires to positive, constructive actions,*
*   thus allowing himself to move into higher energy*
*   vibrations and evolve to spiritualization which*
*   brings true joy and eternal life.*
He can become an instrument to help people
*   understand their true nature and free themselves*
*   from blind suffering and ignorance.*

Your evolution or devolution depends on the subtle
*   movement of the mind.*
Respect this divine instrument and use it well.
After refining the mind to more subtle levels,
*   one can experience the Subtle Origin of the universe*
*   and thus the origin of one's own existence.*
The Subtle Origin is formless.

It is made of no-thing, but from this nothing
*   all existence comes into being.*
This no-thing of the universe is creative
*   and constructive energy.*
If you keep your mind in this nothing,
*   which in its very nature is being,*
*   you imitate the process of the universe.*

You will flow on the stream of creative
and constructive energy and all your
positive thoughts will come true.

This energy flows from the origin of the universe,
from the origin of your true mind.
Keep your mind still without coming or going
and you will be one with Tao.
You will know that your own energy
is the energy of the universe and that the
universal spirit is your own true spirit.
This spirit is all-powerful, all-creative,
and can penetrate the material world.
Since it is formless and has no substance,
there are no obstacles in its way.
Nothing can harm it.
It can come or go as it wishes.
This spirit, as your true nature, can float in space.
In the morning it can roam over the earth,
and at night sleep in the Heavenly realms.
Boundless space is its home, your home.

* * * * *

First, gain control of the body and all its organs.
Then control the mind and attain one-pointedness.
The harmony of Heaven will then come to dwell within you.
You will be radiant with life.
You will rest in Tao.
You will have the simple look of a newborn calf.
O, lucky you.
You will not even know the cause of your state.

The Realization of Eternal Existence
Follow the method of self-cultivation and connect
*   yourself with the supreme sovereign of the universe.*
The divine spirits will then authorize your
*   self-cultivation and help you on the path of Tao.*
When you can combine your energy
*   with their subtle energy, you imitate Heaven*
*   and all your deeds become pure.*
You will spread your spiritual energy
*   as an offering to help mankind.*
Your positive energy can permeate all Heavens and Earth.
All divine energies are in their correct position
*   and communicate their magnificence to your cultivation.*
They will pass down the highest wisdom.
After you have attained your self-realization
*   your true nature will shine forth.*
You will have sovereignty over nature
*   and complete dominion over the physical world*
*   and your own life.*
Refine your physical body until its coarse energy
*   becomes exquisite spiritual energy.*
In this way you will reach eternal life.

* * * * *

All that is limited by form, semblance,
    sound and color is called object.
Among them all,
    man alone is more than an object.
Though like objects he has form and semblance,
    he is not limited to form, he is more.
He can attain formlessness.
When he is beyond "this" and "that,"
    where is the comparison with another object,
    where is the conflict?
He will rest in his eternal place,
    which is no place.
He will be hidden in his own unfathomable secret.
His nature sinks to its root in the One.
His vitality, his power, hide in the secret Tao.

Heaven does nothing;
> its non-doing is its serenity.

Earth does nothing;
> its non-doing is its rest.

From the union of these two non-doings,
> all actions proceed
> and all things are made.

How vast, how invisible this coming to be!
All things come from nowhere.
How vast, how invisible,
> no way to explain it.

All beings in their perfection
> are born of non-doing.

Hence it is said,
> Heaven and Earth do nothing,
> yet there is nothing they do not do.

Where is the person
> who can attain this non-doing?

* * * * *

Does Tao exist?
Can it not exist?
Is there a thing that exists that does not exist?
To name Tao is to name no-thing.
Tao is not the name of an existence.
Cause and chance have no bearing on Tao.
Tao is a name that indicates without defining.
Tao is beyond words and beyond things.
It is not expressed either in word or in silence.
Where there is no longer word or silence,
> Tao is apprehended.

The achieved one remains unknown.
Perfect virtue produces nothing.
No-self is true self.
And the greatest person is nobody.

In embracing the One with your soul,
    can you never forsake the Tao?
In controlling your vital force
    to achieve gentleness,
    can you become like a newborn child?
In cleansing and purifying your mystic vision
    can you strive for perfection?

* * * * *

Fish are born in water,
    a person is born in Tao.
If fish seek the deep shadow of pond and pool,
    all their needs are satisfied.
If a person sinks into the deep shadow of non-action,
    forgetting aggression and concern,
    he lacks nothing and his life is secure.
All a fish needs is to get lost in water.
All a person needs is to get lost in Tao.

* * * * *

The productive power
    of the universe never dies.
It is called the Mystic Female.
The door of the Mystic Female
    is the root of Heaven and Earth.
Continuously, continuously,
    it seems to remain.
Draw upon it and it serves you with ease.

Chapter 6

The Golden Collection
of Spiritual Practices, Part I

Innermost Spiritual Practices and Invocations

Before reading and using these invocations, it is necessary to have a basic understanding of the purpose of this section of the book. These ancient invocations are treasures of the Integral Way, and through their diligent practice your mind may be strengthened and your spirit integrated.

The core of the integral spiritual realm of an individual or of the entire universe is an inexpressible, indescribable stillness. However, it has a subtle, inexhaustible movement which can be traced by following the harmonious, gentle pulsations of the integral spiritual realm in its clarity and distinction. The integralness of spiritual reality is revealed in these invocations and they are an important practice for those who wish to proceed in their spiritual development.

In spiritual practice, an auxiliary measure to assist an individual in attaining Tao is the practice of clear thinking and clear language. It is not like other traditions in which strange sounds and vibrations are considered to be high spiritual phenomena, and whose practices further imitate such strange phenomena.

In other traditions, loud repetition of these strange sounds and prayers are emphasized. In natural spiritual practice, reading or praying with the mind is valued. Why? Because in spiritual reality, thinking is louder than thunder. This is one of the great truths in spiritual practice. Thus, using the invocations in this book with a clear mind, and reading them distinctly with the mind, is the correct and effective way to proceed.

These sacred invocations are based upon the universal subtle law of energy correspondence and the response and attraction of energy. Their purpose is to cause the response of the divine energy of the highest and subtlest realms of the universe, which is the direct origin of the mainstream of ancient, prehistoric Tao.

Through causing the response of the universal energies, it is possible first of all to prove for yourself the existence of subtle spiritual beings. These divine beings exist for all people, but not all people can prove their existence. It is also possible to experientially determine your level of evolution, based on the energy which responds to you.

Through utilizing the invocations, you will be able to experience higher and subtler realms of being and unite these energies with your own corresponding internal energies. Unification with higher universal energies will confer upon you harmony with and sovereignty over nature.

Diligent and consistent practice of these invocations will positively reform your mind and mold your spirit. The ultimate goal of the invocations is the realization of the eternal Tao as your own true nature. With this realization, you can completely merge your being with the Tao.

In order to benefit from the invocations, it is necessary to have spiritual purity or chastity, and devotion to the universal Integral Way of spiritual development. With this in mind, you need to make a clear decision about how to proceed with your spiritual cultivation and also how to choose from all the connected spiritual disciplines in your life. If you are not ready to make this spiritual self-commitment to the universal Divine Realm, and do not have the highest respect for these invocations and the divine message they represent, then using them casually will only harm your true nature.

These invocations are for your protection and the well-being and capability of your soul. Even natural people need to be equipped with good tools to respond to different situations. These invocations were not created by any one person; they have true traditional value.

Essentially, there are three types of invocations. One type expands your range to reach the most subtle level. Practicing these invocations will bring about the breakthrough of conceptual limitations. The second type is for spiritual cultivation. These invocations help you to gather and refine spiritual energy to integrate your subtle body. The third type of invocation is practical and can be used to attain spiritual stability and purity. At the same time, these invocations can fortify your mental vibration, especially after physical exuviation, when you have transformed your physical body and your spirit carries the seed of your life.

Here are some general suggestions to make these invocations more serviceable. Once you become used to reciting them, the practice should change from being formal to being formless. Before sleeping and when you wake up, or anytime while your mind is overactive, these practices can be done voicelessly, with no formality. By no formality, I mean there is no need for postures, such as sitting upright. Of course it is not suitable to practice them when you use the toilet, are menstruating or engaging in something that is not decent. I hope that you are achieved enough to know when and where it is suitable to do certain things.

Practicing these invocations builds spiritual dignity and sublimity. Although in the spiritual world, every being is equal, some are more powerful and more sublime because of how they train or treat themselves.

Statement of Sincerity

I search only for the most refined divine energy
which reveals itself as the Heavenly Way.
I am willing to follow the way of universal nature
and renounce all distorted images and descriptions.
I do not doubt the truth of natural beings,
just as I do not doubt my own being.
My life is the Heavenly Way itself
which dwells in this world.
I respect my life and all other lives as well.
I lead my life in obedience
to the cosmic law of life.
I will never violate the heavenly, responsive,
Universal Law of Harmony.
Nor will I damage my life by ignorant behavior
or negative thoughts.

PURIFICATIONS

The purifying invocations should be done before any of the circulatory practices and should precede the Requests and Enrichments. Beginning with the Purification of the Mouth, do each Purification for seven days and then <u>add</u> the next one in order. (First Week - Purification of the Mouth; Second Week - Purification of the Mouth and Purification of the Body; Third Week - Purification of the Mouth, Purification of the Body, and Purification of the Mind, etc.)

The Purification of the Earth can be used when offending the earth, such as pulling up a tree, or other work in the earth, or around the area of the Shrine. Rough or noisy work like vacuuming or using chemical cleaners, etc. can usually be done before a place is used as a shrine or a quiet room. Afterwards, the cleaning is best done manually so that it does not disturb the energy.

The "Purification of My Entire Being in Union with Heaven and Earth" may be used to cleanse the unpleasant or frightening shadow remaining from the experience of a bad dream and prevent its occurrence in the physical realm of life. It may also be used when there is sickness in the home or when mysterious sounds are heard.

To be effective, Purifications must be practiced diligently and properly with good concentration and sincerity.

The Five Purifications

When Tao reveals itself through the mouth,
it manifests as the God of the Mouth.
When Tao reveals itself through the body,
it manifests as the God of the Body.
When Tao reveals itself through the mind,
it manifests itself as the God of the Mind.
When Tao reveals itself through the earth
it manifests itself as the God of the Earth.
When Tao reveals itself through your entire being
it manifests itself as the God of your Entire Being.
Tao makes itself evident through its infinite variations,
but in truth it is One.

Purification of the Mouth
God of the Mouth, Dan Chu, door guardian of my body,
gather only positive energy.
Goddess of the Tongue, Ching Luen,
nurture my in-coming and out-going energy,
and connect my being to the divine realm of the universe.
God of the Teeth, Luo Chien,
refine the coarseness and protect the true nourishment
of my body and mind.
God of the Throat, Hu Fen,
be the pathway for constructive energy only,
and induce refined saliva as "Jade Dew."
Goddess of Thought, Shih Shen,
maintain stability, straighten your activity,
and continue the refinement of my life.
All Gods and Goddesses,
help me to achieve the pure energy of the Heavenly Way
that is everlasting.
So it is commanded and confirmed.

Purification of the Body
With the sun I wash my body.
With the moon I refine my form.
With the divine immortals I am supported.
With the eternal beings I perpetuate my own eternal life.
I unite myself with the enduring energy
of the twenty-eight constellations.
Within and without, all impurities are cleansed
with divine water.
Most respected heavenly divinity,
console my body.
Saturate my souls and energy with the light
of all stars in the enormous "bushel" of space.
Eastern stars of the "Green Dragon,"
lead me forward.
Western stars of the "White Tiger,"
protect me from behind.
Southern stars of the "Red Bird,"
guard me from above.
Northern stars of the "Black Turtle,"
guard me from below.
So it is commanded and confirmed.

Purification of the Mind

Divine stars of the three terraces,
symbols of my three yang souls,
respond to my spiritual progress,
and unceasingly drive away
negative energy and demons.
Protect my life and guard my body.
Help me commune with the Divine Immortals.
I dedicate myself to serve the eternal Heavenly Way.
Help me attain crystal clear wisdom
and a universal heart.
Return my mind to its original innocence.
Refresh my souls so I may express only positivity.
Straighten my energy so my spirit will grow
without hindrance.
So it is commanded and confirmed.

Purification of the Earth

Most responsive Divinity of my altar,
and all celestial and terrestrial spirits,
assist me in communicating with
all Heavens and Earths.
Help me pass through the world of form
and the world of no form with complete freedom.
Do not hesitate to guard me.
Help me to restore
my inner cosmic order and overcome
my habitual inertia and chaos.
With this merit you will share in my cultivation.
Join in my divine nature and save me from falling.
So it is commanded and confirmed.

Purification of My Entire Being
in Union With Heaven and Earth

Heavens and Earths are spontaneous manifestations
of the wondrous universal law.
As the original Oneness expresses itself,
gross and subtle energy become distinguished.
My Bodily Cave is brightly illumined
by the mysterious light of my three Tan Tiens,
the bridge points to immortality.
The powerful spirits of the eight directions
unite my being with the true origin of life.
By the unalterable order of the divine treasure
in the Ninth Heaven,
send the protective divine energy of
Chien Lou, Dan Na, Dun Kan and T'ai Shuan
to destroy my spiritual obstacles
and eliminate any evil influences.
This divine notice is given by the central summit
to all natural sovereigns.
These precious words come from the Subtle Origin.
With them, I express my strong determination
to drive away all demons and evil
in order to strengthen my health
and lengthen my years.
Spirits of the Five Authoritative Mountains,
rulers of all the plains, respond to me.
Spirits of all the seas, take notice.
Demon king, Mu Wang, you are chained
and stand guard as my servant.
A harmonious atmosphere is within and around me.
The energy of the Heavenly Way is everlasting.
So it is commanded and confirmed.

Mountains, as natural formations, symbolize high spiritual achievement. In fact, the peak of a mountain gathers more natural energy than lower places. For this reason, the ancient achieved ones would usually dwell in the high mountains to cultivate themselves and gather this energy in order to achieve themselves. In this invocation, the term "central summit" symbolizes the highest natural peak, and

also the highness of your spiritual scope. The "Five
Authoritative Mountains" are arranged with the highest
mountain in the center and the others as the four corners.
Each mountain has its own good energy, but the highest in
the middle is the most powerful. This corresponds with Kun
Lun, the highest spiritual mountain in China. In our body
it symbolizes the top of our head, which can also gather
high energy.

All human beings are born generally equal, with some
energy differences. Some energy is higher, some lower.
After achievement, your level is different. Then you have
reached the highest peak of spirit.

DAILY PRACTICES

Invocation of Burning Incense

*I cultivate myself and follow the Heavenly Way
    with a lucid mind and subtle energy.
With this incense, I connect my whole being
    with that of all Divine Immortals.
Incense is burned in this beautiful censer
    so that I may present my spirit and mind
    to the highest realm of universal integration.
Eyes of the divine spirits,
    gaze upon my heart and reflect my devotion to the truth.
Subtle light of the Divine Immortals,
    shine upon this earthly altar
    and make my energy divine and effective.
I request the highest divine energy of Heaven
    to respond to me.
I humbly offer this sincere petition
    through the fragrant vibration of this incense.*

This invocation is used when offering incense or
perfumed oil. It may be done for three days prior to
beginning the Purifications, or when presenting yourself
before the Shrine. It may also be used after a bad dream.

Always burn incense vertically. Use only high quality incense or aromatic oil, not overly strong sweet-smelling products which cause too much stimulation.

Daily Mental Discipline

I am the offspring of the divine nature of the universe.
Through the positive, creative and constructive
nature of the universe I have been given life.
May pure, positive energy display itself
in my nature and in my daily life.
May only the highest energy manifest
in my speech and my behavior.
May I demonstrate the benevolence of universal nature
in my relationships with my fellow men and women.
May pure, positive energy
be the only reality of my being.
May my spirit and mind reflect
the sublime harmony and order of the universe,
and may my body be a workshop of the subtle origin.
When I have a meal,
may pure, positive energy nourish me.
When I sleep,
may a peaceful nature refresh me.
When I work,
may the exppression of the Divine Nature be my task.
When I conduct my life,
may Universal Nature be my only way.

This invocation is suitable for daily use and is best used in the morning hours. It can reform your daily life and help you in the conduct of your life.

REQUESTS

Request for Heavenly Energy

I request the divine energy of Heaven to respond to me.
When it responds,
I am inspired by everything around me.
I faithfully follow the Way of Heaven
by keeping my mind pure and single-purposed.
If my mind is pure and single-purposed,
Heaven will enlighten me.
The Heavenly Way transmits itself
through my divine nature.
As the divine nature unfolds,
sacred practices can enlighten my mind.
Heaven is responsive.
Earth is responsive.
Mankind is responsive.
I now request the most exalted divine energy
of the universe, and all the Divine Immortals
and all Heavenly beings to accept me as their friend
so that my body will be spiritually responsive,
so that my speech will be spiritually responsive,
so that my volition will be spiritually responsive.
Thus I will be able to follow the Heavenly Way
wholeheartedly and transmit it without hesitation.
So it is commanded and confirmed.

Request to All Pure Spirits

My refined energy becomes like jade and gold
as it connects with the highest subtle energy,
inviting the noblest purple light
to envelop the shrine of my body.
With my positive breath I extend protection
to all beings in order to realize
my true divine nature.
I use all my power so that this humble intention
will be realized.
T'ai Chi begins with Oneness,
and contains my essence and my spirit.

The supernatural power of all the Divine Immortals
supports me as well as the boundless grace
of the highest realm of universal integration.
The Heavenly Way encompasses all beings impartially.
Divine energy is more subtle than smoke or fire
My refined yin energy transforms as jade girls
spreading beautiful flowers.
My refined yang energy transforms as golden boys
spreading my good wishes.
I request all high pure spirits to present themselves.
Heavenly majesty envelops this shrine
that resides under the starry sky.
The subtle energy that exists everywhere
is effective and responsive.
With my subtle invocation I can touch
the divine, ultimate truth.
All spirits are sensitive to this invocation.
With my head raised in sincere expectation,
I respectfully request all pure spirits
to use my cultivation as a spiritual shelter.
My heart is open like a huge valley,
only Tao fills its center.
I employ this invocation so that my selfless
intentions will actualize.
The subtle divine energy responds.
So it is commanded and confirmed.

The Requests should be done consistently and with good concentration starting with the Request for Heavenly Energy for 49 days, and then doing both of them for 49 days. These invocations entreat Heavenly energy to unite with and assist you in becoming spiritually responsive.

ENRICHMENTS

The Enrichments should be done for 49 days each. Begin with the Enrichment from the Integral Spiritual Realm and after 49 days, do the Enrichment from the Integral Spiritual Realm and the Enrichment from the Divine Origin of the Universe. Continue, adding the third and fourth enrichments after each 49-day period.

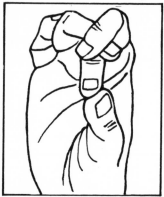

Note: When doing the Enrichment for All Elements of My Being, face south. The hands should be in the following positions: The right hand should be in the thunder position which is made by curling the ring finger over the middle finger, and then curling the index finger over the ring and middle finger. The little finger curls over the ring finger and the thumb supports the middle finger.

The Thunder Position
(Figure 1)

The left hand is in the sword position which is made by extending the index finger and middle finger together while holding the other two fingers with the thumb.

Both hands should rest on the knees while sitting in the cross-legged position.

The Sword Position
(Figure 2)

Enrichment from the Integral Spiritual Realm
The divine realm of universal integration
enlightens my mind and lengthens my years.
The powerful guiding light
of the star shining on my path
cuts through all negative influences.

It illumines my way and nourishes my soul
    so that my positive energy is always integrated.
In this way my life is long and harmonious.
No evil force can enter my body or mind,
    thus the normalcy and well-being of my life are ensured.
My body is strengthened.
My mind is well balanced,
    allowing me to remain steadfast
    in the Heavenly Way.
As I am enriched by the divine nature of the universe,
    I continue to grow into the Realms of Purity.

Enrichment from the Divine Origin of the Universe

From Heaven the chi of purity descends.
From Earth the chi of harmony ascends.
The energy of Heaven and Earth have intercourse.
I receive my life full of divine energy
    with which my sincere soul is strengthened,
    and my humble mind is enlightened.
My body and mind, my essence and spirit,
    unite with universal yin and yang.
All positive and constructive elements
    in the virtuous realms quickly respond
    to this invocation and unite with me.
Divine Immortals fly among auspicious clouds
    in the vastness of space
    and give me a ride.
Truly achieved beings come to greet
    the refined essence of my being.
The divine energy of Heaven is boundless
    and supernatural.
As I receive the highest enrichment
    from the divine life source of the universe,
    I unite with the precious divine energy
    and preserve it both within and without.

Enrichment From the Highest Realm
of Universal Integration

The Way of Heaven arms me with strong
positive energy as my subtle weapon.
With this energy I can sweep away
any corruption and clear my path.
The divine integrity of the universe has sent me
to take this form of life
in order to carry out my Heavenly vocation
of promoting upliftment;
of expanding safety and purity;
of spreading pure culture to the masses;
of influencing people to cooperate;
and of replacing armies with peaceful means.
With this enrichment I extend peace in all directions.
I eliminate all negative forces.
No evil can hide from my natural surveillance.
All of my positive intentions can be achieved,
from beginning to end.
Enriched by the highest realm of universal integration,
I protect my virtuous being
and all creatures and all nations.

Enrichment of All Elements of My Being

A clear mind is the master of my being.
To my left, "The Green Dragon" regenerates
the energy of my liver.
To my right, "The White Tiger" purifies
the energy of my lungs.
To my front, "The Red Bird" vitalizes
the energy of my heart.
At my back, "The Black Turtle" restores
the energy of my kidneys and bladder.
To be content and happy is the function of my spleen.
To explore and be free is the function of my mind.
To be active yet serene is the function of my body.
To perceive brightness is the function of my eyes.
To hear sounds is the function of my ears.

To take in vital energy is the function of my mouth
    and nostrils.
To express the truth is the function of my tongue.
To cut and chew is the function of my teeth.
To enjoy peace is the energy of my gall.
To work and create is the energy of my hands.
To move and dance is the function of my feet.
To cling and unite is the function of my desires.
Forests and trees correspond to the energy of my hair.
Rivers and waterways correspond to my intestines.
Lakes and seas correspond to my abdomen.
All good energies flow to Kuan Yuan's vital origin,
    the center of my lower abdomen,
    in my lower Tan Tien.
Correct functioning and positive energy
    are expressed through each organ.
Every part of my body corresponds
    to every part of the universe.
Before the manifestation of my life,
    T'ai Chi is the origin.
After my birth, Heaven and Earth become separated.
I have the duty of self-reintegration.
I merge with the great Tao.
Once my energy is cultivated and refined,
    I will find assistance if there is difficulty,
    and help if there is resistance.
If I am in harmony with the natural functioning
    of the universe,
    when I look for help
    positive energy will respond to me.
The sublimation and refinement of my essence
    brings the opportunity to ascend
    to the highest Heavens.
This authority is given to me
    by the integral spiritual realm
    of universal purification and integration.

Alternate Version of
Enrichment of All Elements of My Being

Goddess of the Mind, be seated on your throne
as the only master of my being.
Goddess of the Liver and Nerves, be my assistant on the left;
support me as the powerful Green Dragon
in the Eastern sky.
Goddess of the Lung and Breath,
be my guardian on the right;
support me as the brave White Tiger
in the Western sky.
Goddess of the Heart, happy and light,
be my guide from in front,
support me as the Red Bird in the Southern sky.
Goddess of the Kidneys and Bladder,
support me from the rear,
as the peaceful Black Turtle in the Northern sky.
Goddess of the Spleen, balance my labor and leisure.
Goddess of Gall Bladder, subdue all evil
and fortify my uprightness.
Goddess of All Souls,
help me attain absolute freedom.
Goddess of Vigor,
adjust to my movement and quietude.
Goddess of the Eyes,
see clearly and gather high spiritual rays.
Goddess of the Ears, hear well the furthest sounds,
and the inspiring Heavenly melody.
Goddess of the Nose,
breathe harmoniously and nurture me.
Goddess of the Mouth and Tongue,
guard me from evil, and attain only good.
Goddess of the Teeth, be strong and firm.
Goddess of the Stomach, digest well and gather essence.
Goddess of the Bowels,
retain the pure and cast off the impure.
Goddess of the Vital Pivot and Tan Tien,
refine my chi.
Goddess of the Hair,
be luxuriant, graceful and communicative.
God of the Spine, support the expansion
of Heaven and Earth as the pillar of the universe.

God of the Shoulder,
    carry the Sun, the Moon, and all Heavenly bodies.
God of the Hand, perform the work of the divine creator.
God of the Feet, move through the universe freely.
God of Respiration, be steady and deep.
God of Chi, be lasting and soft.
All thirty-six thousand gods of my life being
    are strongly united.
All thirty-six thousand gods manifest the truth of oneness.
The powerful stars of the Big Dipper
    dwell in the orifices of my head.
The twenty-eight constellations settle on my body.
All high spiritual beings, be with me.
I refine myself to attain reunion with the divine Primal Chi.
With the confirmation of my will,
    the divine Primal Chi makes these all possible.
I transcend the dusty world,
    break through the obstinacy of my ignorance,
    destroy all disguised obstacles,
    and dissolve all difficulties in my way.
I turn all misfortunes into blessings,
    and correct the ominous to be auspicious.
I gather all blessings by way of Tao.
May it be as commanded and confirmed.

HARMONIZATIONS

The Spiritual Harmonizations should be done for seven days each beginning with the Spiritual Harmonization with the Sun. After doing this invocation for seven days, do the Spiritual Harmonization with the Sun and the Spiritual Harmonization with the Moon, each for seven days. Next do all three of the Spiritual Harmonizations for seven days.

Spiritual Harmonization With the Sun

As the luminous energy of the sun shines in the East,
*   I unite with its pure yang energy*
*   and am empowered to eliminate all negativity.*
All ghosts and demons immediately disappear.
There is nothing I cannot see,
*   and nothing that can stop me.*
Water cannot drown pure yang.
Fire cannot harm pure yang.
Of all spheres of life, pure yang is the most precious.
I harmonize with the luminous
*   and glorious sun in the East forever.*

The Spiritual Harmonization with the Sun should be done in the day time. This invocation can help confirm your spiritual authority and may be used when helping people.

Spiritual Harmonization With the Moon

Shining in the West, the clear, pure moon is waxing,
*   splendid and bright.*
Shining in the dark sky, it is so lucid and full
*   it cannot be covered by a single bit of dust.*
By its illumination, negativity is dispersed.
Assisting the yang with the yin,
*   only lucidity can give birth to light,*
*   only the pure can achieve effectiveness of spirit.*
I harmonize with the clear, pure Moon in the sky.

This invocation should be done when the moon is shining brightly at night.

Spiritual Harmonization With Great Nature

My divine nature is as pure as the nature of Heaven.
The constancy of my strength is like the Sun.
The lucidity of my mind is as bright as the Moon.
My tolerance is like that of the good Earth.
My forwardness is effortless, like flowing water.
My calmness is like the mountains.

I preserve the Heavenly order above,
the Earthly order below,
and the order of the myriad beings in the middle.
I trust in Tao and follow the Eternal Way.
Without excess, a human life is naturally long.
I unite with the profundity of Nature.
I renew my relationship with the maternal
and paternal energies of the universe.

INVOCATIONS

Communion With the Jade Emperor

Your sublime energy envelops all Heavens.
It is the wonderful and mysterious source of energy rays
which extend throughout the universe.
Your divine authority over this gold and purple shrine
in my head makes it the most glorious palace on earth.
You are the Primal Energy and the most exquisite
of all beings.
You can be measured only by infinity.
You are the source of subtle light, purity, quietude
and impartiality.
You support all dimensions through your virtuous example.
The Divine Immortals are extensions of your
subtle energy.
Your comprehensive wisdom is quiet, pure and profound.
Your calmness is sublime.
To settle arguments through arguing
is not your way.
Your way is simplicity.
Your power is sincerity.
Your paternal energy sires selflessness.
Your maternal energy gives birth to kindness.
You reach fullness through emptiness.
The completeness of your virtue
supports those who are incomplete in virtue.

You take no measure of individual beingness.
Your absolute comprehensiveness contains all existence.
You are the essential result of the highest sublimation.
You are the eternal guide of the unfolding universe.
You are the generator of the Eternal Way.
A thousand beautiful cultures of humanity seek you
      and attempt to describe you.
You set the untamed world in order
      with your subtle formulas.
You preserve the truth on the physical pathway
      by combining the physical with the spiritual.
The Purple Tower Palace in the Heaven of my heart
      is your residence.
The coarsest places of earth are also your workshop.
You ride on a white energy horse,
      running in the channel of time and space.
The most mysterious places of all
      are also your altar.
You communicate with all beings
      in all realms of existence.
You reside not only in the yellow and gold source
      of the highest Heaven, but also in the lowest
      places of the Earth.
You encompass all beings within your boundless tolerance.
You are the unruling master of the profound vastness.
With my mouth, my body, my will and my whole heart,
      I return to you.
I will follow Tao for all eternity.

The Jade Emperor is the directing energy of the universe. The Communion With the Jade Emperor, The God of Jade Light, should be done in the morning. It is an invocation for general use and is practiced for spiritual centering and enhancing positive energy.

The Golden Light Invocation
*The mysterious origin of Heaven and Earth
  is the source of pure energy.
With this energy we can rectify imbalances
  and communicate with the entirety.
Within and without the three spheres of the universe,
  only Tao is most revered.
From Tao I receive subtle Golden Light
  to envelop and protect my body and soul.
It is so subtle that it cannot be seen or heard.
The subtle Golden Light permeates Heaven, Earth and me.
It nourishes and educates all life.
I utter this heavenly invocation with deep sincerity.
Spiritual beings, guard me.
High deities of the Five Directions,
  assist me.
Divine Immortals, kindly accept me.
The Golden Light enables me to transcend
  all worldly troubles.
I am given power over all evil forces.
Enlightenment comes from the Divine Immortals
  like thunder breaking through dark clouds.
They inspire the clarity and wisdom
  to see through all obstacles.
My upright chi is shining and active.
May the Jade Marrow of Heaven fill my bones.
May the holy medicine of immortality grow within me.
May spiritual resources always reach me.
I truly know the holy medicine of immortality
  that is colorless and flavorless.
After 10,000 repetitions of this invocation,
  the wonderful secrets of all supernatural beings
  will become self-evident to me.
Jade Emperor, Everlasting One of the Universe,
  may your Golden Light descend and guide me.*

The generation of golden light creates an effective protection, mentally as well as spiritually and physically. The "Golden Light Invocation" is practiced to begin nurturing the golden light as your own protective power or energy transformation. When it becomes strong enough, it will be the best protection for you and for those who have not lost the ability to be spiritually receptive. After reading this invocation, inhale golden light into the lower *Tan Tien*, then visualize golden light surrounding the whole body. The saliva should then be swallowed and applied to the five directions. Do this practice in the morning for 49 days.

Invocation of Dual Cultivation

Peace in all aspects of my life
   originates from my sexual performance.
I turn away from the basic pattern of animals.
I do not fight.
I do not kill.
I do not engage in conquering through war.
My peaceful sexual performance
   brings peace to all areas of my life.
Friction brings only short-lived rejoicing,
   and leaves irritability and anger
   in all relationships.
In my subtle performance,
   I am receptive and cooperative,
   and let happiness come from consonant union.
It is not fighting that brings unison.
Unison completes itself.
It is not making love that brings love,
   it is love which ignites
   the harmony of life.
Through my balanced work of harmonization,
   the yin and yang of the universe are united.
Fire and Water assist each other.
Mercury and Lead stabilize each other.
Kun and Li support each other.
Metal and Wood cease fighting each other.
Sun and Moon converge.
Wuh earth (man's heart) and Shr earth (woman's heart)
   mold each other.
All relationships in my life,
   and all relationships in the world
   are harmoniously fulfilled and realized.

Suggestion for practice: In *The Complete Works of Lao Tzu*, see the Chapters Sixty-seven to Seventy-three of the "Hua Hu Ching" for instruction on dual cultivation. Also refer to *Harmony: The Art of Life.*

Instruction From the Jade Emperor
on How to Become a Divine Immortal
(First Version)

The Sacred Immortal Medicine has three components: *ching, chi and shen*, which are located in specific areas of the body. Because they are invisible and subtle, the correct way must be followed to cultivate them.

First, eliminate the abuse of your mind, and then the three subtle elements can grow undisturbed. If you follow the practice of integrating these three into one, with the help of the breathing system, eventually your work will become effective. In this way you will be able to have a real audience with the Everlasting One, the Jade Emperor, face to face. If the internal work is diligently performed for years, you will be able to ascend to the Heavenly realms. For the wise this is easy to understand, but for the foolish it is impossible to accept.

Every morning at dawn you should unite with the harmonious light available at that time. As you inhale, the vitalizing *chi* and its purity enter your body. After inhaling this *chi* from the sun, exhale all of the impure, black *chi* within you. Do this with a relaxed mind, employing little rigid control. Do it as if you were not doing it, following the principle of being natural. Gently keep the delicate energy within yourself, and experience the nourishing clarity. In this way the eternal fruit will grow, and the root will reach deeper and deeper in the universe.

Each individual is gifted by nature with his own *ching.* Unite your *ching* with *shen.* Unite shen with *chi.* Then unite your *chi* with the Primal *chi* of the universe. This is the true realization of immortality in which every moment is a new life. If this wondrous truth is not understood, all of the sacred books become meaningless.

The *shen*, because of its subtlety, is the highest power and can penetrate all things. *Shen* can fly from its form. *Shen* cannot be drowned in water or burned in fire. For now, your *shen* depends on your body to stabilize it.

When the *ching* is full, the *chi* also becomes full. Like an evergreen, you must grow your *ching* and *chi*. In this way your life's tree will never wither, even when reaching your "winter" years. *Ching*, *chi* and *shen* are in fact one. To find this wonderful miracle, you need only know this precious treasure within your being.

Heaven is too wonderful to be understood with the vulgar mind. If you can avoid this pitfall of your own narrow thinking and follow this oracle, you will realize the total integration of your being. Also remember that only when *chi* has been accumulated can you cultivate the Sacred Immortal Medicine. When the *chi* is scattered, there is no hope of doing this.

Through the cultivation of *ching*, *chi* and *shen*, your seven upper orifices will radiate out the beautiful light from deep within you. The sun and moon will shine within you.

Once you achieve success in your cultivation, the result is eternity. Your body will be light and your elements will be harmonious. Jade marrow will fill your bones. If you succeed, this Sacred Immortal Medicine, the goal of your cultivation, will certainly be achieved. If you fail to obtain the Sacred Immortal Medicine, your energy resources will eventually become exhausted and you will be bound to your biological destiny. This sacred medicine is to be found within your own body, but its subtlety is beyond the perception of black and white.

If you read this invocation time after time, the subtle meaning of its wonderful principle will become apparent to you. It is the true practice, paralleled with virtue, by which you may achieve preparation for immortality.

(Second Version)
The precious Immortal Medicine is contained within you:
  shen as spirit and mind,
  chi as general vitality,
  and ching as sexual energy.
They are one energy manifested in different forms.
To maintain integrity, do not employ them in isolation.
Before manifestation, this high potency of life
  is whole and subtle.
In your cultivation, return to the subtle breath
  before you were born.
After a certain length of time, wholeness can be seen;
  it will become the foundation of your spiritual empire.
You then can have a personal audience with
  the Jade Emperor who sits firmly on the throne within.
With him, you ride on the natural cycle of universal energy
  and are able to ascend from the lower sphere of nature
  to the high Heavenly realms.
For the person of high intelligence,
  this is easy to fulfill;
  but for the ignorant it is difficult to accept.
In the early morning's dawn,
  inhale and exhale the clarity and purity.
Like the fetus,
  rest in the mysterious womb of the mother.
In this way you gather your own subtle essence
  and enjoy steady subtle growth.
As the integrity of your life is restored,
  you will find the true fulfillment of immortality;
  all things are only temporarily named.
The truth of immortality is dependent
  on your integrated new life of wholeness.
Your integrated new life of wholeness
  is able to penetrate the densest stones
  and soar freely in the ethereal sky.
This integrated new life cannot be drowned,
  nor can it be burned in the hottest fire.
In general, spirit must integrate with form,
  subtle essence depends on vital chi.

Once achieved, it becomes undecaying and unwithering,
  like an evergreen.
In the beginning these three are not separate;
   as one, their subtle power is beyond the mind's grasp.
Only when they are completely integrated
  do we have the precious Immortal Medicine.
When they are separated, there is no power.
For the achieved one,
    the seven orifices communicate with each other,
    each imparting its own subtle light.
Once you gain immortality,
   your body becomes light.
Your inner Sun and Moon will shine
   in the "Golden Court" of your life being.
You will glow with an auspicious light
   and be filled with the most precious harmony.

(Third Version)
The best medicine is not far away;
   spirit, vigor and sexual stamina are all within you.
Through the non-controlling refinement process
   of evasiveness and elusiveness,
   the medicine becomes real
   when one keeps an unoccupied mind
   and is mindful of being in the present moment.
When the mind blends with your harmonious breath,
   the medicine naturally becomes effective
   in a hundred days, and the foundation
   of your spiritual empire is built.
Day and night, quietly audience the Divine One,
   the Immortal Emperor within your being.
In twelve years, a natural cycle,
   you attain immortality and transcend
   the bondage of form.
Rise at dawn and nurture yourself with fresh air;
   the foul is naturally exhaled.
The vitalizing essence enters through inhalation;
   it needs no tension, but requires true constancy.
Then the stem of life becomes firm, the root deep.

This is easy to teach the wise,
but difficult for the foolish to understand.
Each person has their own essence.
The true Way is to integrate vigor, sexual stamina and spirit.
If one does not achieve this,
then one's achievement is unreal.
The newly integrated spiritual one
can enter stones, elevate the body,
enter water without being drowned,
and pass through fire without being burned.
One's spirit depends upon form to obtain its life.
Sexual stamina depends upon vigor to become full.
The subtle integration of these three
keep one fresh and unwithered, like the evergreen.
The three have only one truth,
so truly wonderful it is.
It comes to be through convergence,
but through scatteredness it is lost.
When it comes to be, all the facial orifices
become communicative and light.
The inner Sun and Moon light up the "Golden Court"
of your being.
Once you have achieved this,
you forever enjoy life,
your body becomes light,
happiness radiates from your core,
and great harmony comes to stay with you.

Invocation to Obtain Divine Immortality
Through Mystic Pregnancy

Ordinary seeds produce ordinary fruit. Through the mystic pregnancy of the divine energy, a Sacred Fetus has hope of being produced. The seed of immortality is not an ordinary seed. It is the most exquisite energy of the Jade Emperor. Descending from above, the undecaying Jade Seed impregnates the humble student's spiritual womb. If you hope to achieve true spiritual immortality, this is the only way.

The process of the mysterious birth of the universe is incessant, and our new life is continuously regenerating. What is observed as life and death is simply the surface of the universal energy spiral advancing and retreating. Thus, it is more important to work on the essence of life instead of the surface of life. When the essence of one's life is gone, the end of one's life is certain.

Subtle spiritual energy is the true origin of life. Gross physical energy is only the form. If you lose both or either spiritual energy or physical energy, you lose life. To keep your spiritual energy, it is necessary to maintain the natural order of the three spheres of energy which are embodied in human beings. The right order is that gross energy is the servant of subtle energy. Gross energy should be refined and sublimated to evolve to spiritual and subtle energy.

Always follow this Heavenly evolutionary order within. The true function of the mind is that of intermediary between the physical and spiritual realms. Do not let your mind go beyond its right position as the go-between of your body and spirit. If you follow the Heavenly order, you will experience true well-being and avoid the disorder and disharmony caused to your true nature by transgressing this universal principle.

The eternal Tao is our inherent nature. The Way is within us all. The way to achieve immortality is first to pacify your own mind. If you succeed in quieting the mind, then everything will follow the great order of universal Nature. The Mystic Intercourse will be wonderfully undertaken. The Mystic Conception will be sure and safe. The Eternal Seed will have the opportunity to miraculously grow and ripen. This is what the precious oracle tells us.

Invocation for Eliminating
Overactive Sexual Desire

Through the cultivation of our subtle energy
we can achieve divine immortality.
The refined energy within us can blossom
to produce a Sacred Fetus of eternal life.
If we keep our essence calm in the lower Tan Tien
the vital energy can be refined to nurture
the duration of our being.
Energy is the reality of life;
when it leaves the form,
its tangibility departs.
In truth, energy never dies,
but merely changes state.
To achieve eternal life,
it is necessary to maintain non-action
and follow the wonderful example
of the Mysterious Mother by embodying
the creative nothingness.
In this way we can cultivate our true spirit and energy.
If the mind wanders, the energy scatters.
If the mind dwells in its proper position,
the energy does the same.
If you want to become an immortal,
your spirit and divine energy must have
Mystic Intercourse.
Your mind must always be steady and undisturbed
so that your energy will not transform
as thoughts and escape.
Then nothing can either go into or come out of
the true vitality.
In this way spirit and divine energy have
Mystic Intercourse in your body,
and Mystic Conception becomes firm and true.
By nourishing the spirit and divine energy
with calmness, the Sacred Fetus will be born
safely into the great Eternity,
and you will fulfill the profound truth
of the universal T'ai Chi.
This is the true path to immortality.

RELATED PRACTICES

To start your journey on the path to divine immortality, the following internal practice is the first step:

Practice thirty-six swallows of saliva, swallowing the energy delicately.

When you spit out the *chi* of evil thoughts, do so smoothly and lightly.

When you inhale positive, regenerating energy, do so gently and continuously. When you sit, stand, lie down, or move in any way at all, you should breathe in this manner so that you can unite mind with body.

The mind must be kept unoccupied, steady and undisturbed. All noisy, crowded and confused environments must be avoided so that your mind will become like a snake coiled in winter sleep in the cave of your body, hiding under the stone of your confirmed spirit.

The food you eat must be pure, so abstain from eating bloody meat. Also, avoid the stimulation from highly spiced, highly processed, and otherwise unnecessary food.

This practice was named "The Breath of Mystic Intercourse." It is the Internal Divine Medicine of true immortality which will not only eliminate illness, but will also lengthen your years. If you maintain the practice of this sacred method, there is no doubt that you will become a Divine Immortal.

Invocation for Reaching Longevity and Divinity
The law of Heaven is clarity.
The law of Earth is peace.
The law of Humanity is calmness.
Through compliance with these inherent laws of Nature,
*   Heaven, Earth and Man can meet one another*
*   and become one.*
All three realms of the universe have the same origin.
I now read this invocation to cause all universal
*   manifestations, both internal and external,*
*   to follow the orderly course*
*   of these three realms of energy.*

It is only when all things return
  to their original order and balance
  of the creative Chien and receptive Kun
  that yin and yang can harmonize each other.
When this harmony is achieved,
  Water energy and Fiery energy can circulate unimpeded.
Then everything returns to the root
  where regeneration takes place.
The Dragon of emotion and the Tiger of desire
  become strongly active
  and yet are absolutely obedient to me.
The central Spirit of the Heart, the master of all,
  performs its duty of commanding
  the vital sublimation.
I refine my saliva and restless body fluids
  to become the peaceful vapor of my super energy.
This energy can then be united with the known
  and unknown reality of the universe.
All evils submit to me and are cleansed.
My whole body achieves a state of perfect balance.
The method for making this excellent medicine
  was passed to me by the Divine Immortals
  who instructed me to utilize my own
  energy and essence.
The laboratory in which the refinement process
  can take place functions
  as the Holy Stove and Cauldron
  and is already within my body.
If I always offer the spirit of my life
  to the eternal Tao, I will achieve
  everlasting life and never become worn out.
When the spiritual fruit of my cultivation is ripe,
  I can fly away to the divine subtle realms,
  as quickly as the edict comes from the
  Jade Emperor of Universal Integrity.

After reading this invocation, practice "Beat the Heavenly Drum" 24 times by placing the palms over the ears in such a way that the fingertips come together at the back of the head. The middle finger snaps over the index finger but never quite hits the back of the head. Next, bite the teeth together 36 times (9 times in front, 9 times on right side, 9 times on the back molars and 9 times on the left side). Then swallow the saliva and *chi* three times, sending it into the lower *Tan Tien.*

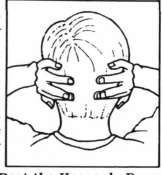

Beat the Heavenly Drum
(Figure 3)

Invocation of Summarization

The true functioning of the universe is beyond the ability of language to describe or the mortal mind to encompass. However, we may attempt to illustrate the subtle truths of the universe by creating models or mental pictures which, although limited, may be helpful in pointing our mind in the direction of the Truth.

When we describe the universe, we unavoidably materialize and solidify it. In the process of description, we create subject and object, thereby entertaining the illusion of duality and destroying the experience of universal oneness.

When we look externally in our search for truth, at best we can only examine small fragments of what we perceive, and from those fragments try to theorize the reality of the whole picture. This external approach to the truth is called "science."

However, through changing the direction of our search from external to internal, we may not only eventually experience the whole truth of the universe, but we may also ultimately experience the reality that the entire universe is embodied within one's own true nature.

Invocation for Internal and External
Spiritual Energy Alignment

Before T'ai Chi is the oneness of the Subtle Origin,
containing all Heavens and earths.
From the heart of the Subtle Origin,
the immutable Jade Emperor,
the divinity of Jade Light,
emanates the most supreme, sublime and harmonious
energy of the universe.
Radiating from the God of Jade Light are all
of the universal sovereigns, natural and supernatural
deities and pure spirits.
Within and without the three planes of existence
there are an uncountable number of
creative Divine Immortals.
The Mysterious Maternal energy of the universe
embraces and nurtures me.
The Gods of the six "Jia" and Goddesses of the six "Ting"
are my link with the primary universal energy.
I am always joining my life with the eternal Source.
The natural deities of the twenty-eight constellations
and the Gods of the nine pivotal stars radiate
their subtle beams as my illumination.
The chi of the Heavenly Generals supports me.
The natural sovereigns of the Five Directions
display their magnificent order within me.
The supreme authority of the universe imparts to me
dominion over my own natural flesh life.
All divine beings assist me in my cultivation
and help me in practicing subtle virtue.
By following the Heavenly Way, my positive energy
can permeate all spheres.
Heavenly energy can evoke my spirit from nothingness
into beingness and return it again to its source.
With divine energy I can perform innumerable
transformations as my actualization
of the universal splendor.
My spirit can go through any difficulty without hindrance.

As a result of my own complete integration,
  I can attain supernatural powers over water,
  fire, and other elements.
I remain unharmed and undaunted.
With the clarity of my mind and integrity of my being
  I can go through clouds and mist
  without going astray.
The grossness of my being has been refined.
The subtleness of my essence has been achieved.
In the morning I may roam to the far end of the universe
  and in the evening I can come back where I started.
I experience peace and contentment everywhere.
I totally unite myself with the divine energy of Tao.
Merging in perfect stillness with the Subtle Origin,
  I enjoy sublime harmony with all realms of the universe
  and achieve fullness and completeness
  of my spiritual being.
With this golden oracle from the supreme realm,
  I hold the sacred map to self-mastery
  and transcend my own fleshly nature.
I actualize the true nature of beingness
  in all aspects of the entire universe.

The Invocation of Summarization should be practiced in the morning for 49 days. While reciting this invocation, you must touch the Heavenly Door line. The Heavenly Door line is the second joint on the ring finger of each hand. Touch it with the thumb of the same hand and rest both hands on the knees.

The Heavenly Door Line
(Figure 4)

**Personal Invocation of a Teacher
of Natural Spiritual Truth**

Divine Realm of the universe,
you are unnameable,
while I am nameable.
You are indefinable,
while I am definable.
You are immeasurable,
while I am measurable.
You are indescribable,
nevertheless, I become your description.
You are inexpressible,
nevertheless, I become your expression.
You are unimaginable,
nevertheless, I become your image.
You are formless,
nevertheless, I become your form.
You are voiceless,
nevertheless, I become your voice.
Only when you and I work together
can the magnificence of the universe
be displayed.

What Is Behind the Spiritual Practices

Primal *Chi,* the Mysterious Mother, is the subtle origin of the universe. From this subtle origin all universal energies proceed, giving birth to Heaven and Earth.

All of the energies of the universe can be categorized as either *yin* or *yang.* *Yang* has positive, active attributes, whereas *yin* has negative, inert attributes. It is through the extension of the original energy from the subtle origin, and the cooperation and interaction of *yin* and *yang,* that all phenomena manifest. This is the fundamental principle of the development of the universe.

In terms of quality, universal energies may be classified as gross, physical energy or subtle, spiritual energy. Both are in balance and develop in parallel. The combination of gross and subtle energy gives birth to mankind, which functions as an intermediary between Heaven and Earth. In other words, it is the union of the spiritual and physical planes which creates the mental plane. Because human beings are composed of both physical and spiritual energy, they have the potential either to evolve upward to become more and more spiritualized, thereby preserving their existence and enjoying freedom, or to devolve downward to become more materialized, the result of which is bondage to the physical realm.

All manifestations in the universe are subject to the Law of Transformation. Consequently there is no certainty for the future of an individual, because his energies are in a constant state of change. Although physical energy appears to be stable, it is not enduring. And although spiritual energy appears to be unstable, it is more enduring. If a person of natural spiritual truth is to be successful in achieving spiritualization, it is necessary to have this basic understanding of the reality of universal beingness.

The Jade Emperor, the Divinity of Jade Light, is the most exquisite energy of the universe whose being is the core of universal life. He is the Subtle Origin of all natural beings and supernatural deities, the source of all highness, purity and wisdom. If one can attain this energy, he can surely achieve Divine Immortality and enjoy eternal life. The Divine Jade Light has the ability to purify many other kinds of energy. It is the goal of self-cultivation to completely unite with the most essential energy, the Divine One of Jade Light.

Extending from the Divinity of Jade Light, the center of the whole sphere of life, are the Divine Immortals, the expressions of divine energy which function as the Divinities of Jade Light. The number of *Shiens*, the Divine Immortals in the universe, is uncountable.

It is possible for a human being to become a *Shien* by refining his gross, physical energy to become more refined, spiritual energy. In this way one can actualize the reality of his eternal being and thereby achieve an eternal existence of joyful freedom rather than being trapped in the mechanical physical realm.

The natural formation of Heaven, the pure *yang* sphere, and the physical universe, the pure *yin* sphere, are manifested from the same source. Radiating from that source are ten high energy beams as the Ten Celestial Stems, and twelve lower energy rays as the Terrestrial Branches. The interaction of the Ten Celestial Stems and Twelve Terrestrial Branches make the multiple things and lives of form, and thus the universe constantly unfolds. At the same time the Celestial Stems become the subtle connection of the entire universe, the Terrestrial Branches become twelve channels of universal physical energy. In other words, from the source, as the energy contracts, the subtle spiritual state of energy is drawn inward. As the energy expands, the grosser physical state of energy is manifested outward.

These ten big spokes and twelve smaller spokes connect with a central hub to form the big wheel of universal energy. Besides the main energy beams and rays there are numerous sub-energy beams and rays which work together to bring forth things of multiple forms. Therefore, the wheel view of the universe expresses the elementary or subtle level, while the network view expresses the energy communication and integration level.

Despite the fact that the energy arrangement is extremely complicated for most people, the interwoven, omni-dimensional energy net of the universe may be followed and comprehended through the high development of one's spiritual capability.

All universal energies are embodied within us and correspond with our own innate energies. By consciously connecting our individual energies with the corresponding energies of the universe we may experience higher and subtler realms of being. With this experience we will be able to prove for ourselves that there is no divine existence beyond our own true nature and we may thereby unite ourselves with the eternal Tao.

Chapter 7

The Golden Collection
of Spiritual Practices, Part II

Postures and Practices
for Spiritual Energy Channeling

Like almost everything about the Integral Way, these postures and practices are not nearly as inscrutable as they may appear. Most are simply natural expressions and applications of a few basic principles. If you accept the premise that man is a microcosm of the macrocosm, and understand the concepts of *yin* and *yang* and the five phases of energy transformation and their corresponding phenomena, you will have a good foundation for understanding Chinese holistic medicine, martial arts, astrology, alchemy, geomancy, etc. To familiarize yourself with these principles, you can refer to my book, *Tao, The Subtle Universal Law.*

All practices and postures are designed to aid in the accumulation, circulation, animation and refinement of our energy into subtler and subtler states, until all gross limitations are dissolved and we merge with the subtle essence of all. Since every aspect of life is simply a different manifestation of energy, in actuality these practices strengthen and refine the entirety of our being.

One's energy arrangement determines one's birth, growth, character and the way one thinks and behaves. The importance of the quality and quantity of energy in everyday living cannot be over-emphasized. Our emphasis on energy is simply the result of the knowledge that man is an energetic being, and that to control and harmonize one's energy is fundamental to living optimally and an absolute prerequisite to developing a spiritual life.

When our energy is abundant, we feel good and life's many irritations do not seem to bother us as much as when our energy is depleted. Since possessing a calm mind is basic to all spiritual practices, the state of stability that comes with sufficient energy is essential. However, all of life's problems are not solved by simply accumulating energy. There is nothing more self-destructive than a person with more energy than they can control. We are only interested in gathering subtle energy, and this entails the avoidance of most forms of what modern students think of as "energy." For instance, a serious student of Tao would never take up running because it stirs up too much gross energy from the lower centers of the body. Nor would they take up weight lifting or calisthenics for the same reason, and also because such forms of exercise tend to dissipate the energy too much. Thus, it is not just a matter of gathering a lot of energy, but of gathering subtle energy, and the exercises in this book are designed to do just that.

Also, since most people are a mixture of about 80% gross energy to 20% subtle, you can see the need to attract as much subtle energy as possible, just to strike a balance. How is this done?

First, find an area where subtle *yang* energy prevails. Remote high mountains have always been preferred by ancient achieved ones. Areas with natural underground springs, surrounded by evergreen trees with mountains to the West and lakes to the East, are ideal for gathering *yang* energy. If one is serious about finding such a place, then a study of the principles of geomancy would be beneficial. Once a spot is located through the use of geomancy (otherwise, any good place may be used) the next step is to associate only with people whose energy is already subtle and refined and whose virtue is steadfast. By living a quiet, simple life, not given to needless dissipation and petty business matters so characteristic of modern life, you will slowly but surely accrue a subtle and powerful reserve.

Another important aspect to these practices is the need to constantly readjust oneself in order to flow with the course of nature. This involves becoming aware of and sensitive to the fact that our internal rhythms are completely interconnected with the entirety of the universe, and thus accommodating ourselves to the yearly, seasonal, monthly, daily and hourly cycles generated by the subtle influence of the Earth, the planets and the stars.

According to the ancient developed ones, there is a cosmic energy cycle that involves the interaction of ten Heavenly influences with twelve Earthly influences in a cycle of sixty combinations which apply to the energy of the year, month, day and hour. For more detailed information on this, you can refer to *The Book of Changes and the Unchanging Truth.*

Seasonal changes are much less complicated than daily or hourly cycles, and require only minor changes such as exercise, diet and sleeping habits. For instance, in Spring and Summer one's activities should harmonize with the outgoing, active, creative cycle, while Fall and Winter activities would be more reserved, with an emphasis on the storage and retention of energy. Diet should always be seasonal, with lighter foods eaten in the summer, and heavier meat dishes served in Winter. Sleeping is usually beneficial with the head pointing East the in Spring and Summer, and West in the Fall and Winter.

The phases of the moon also influence spiritual practices. There is a general condition of low energy around the time of no moon, and a period of greater excitation around the Full Moon. The moon also influences sexual practices. For instance, the second day of full moon is the only day of the month men can have sex without damaging their *Ching* (essence).

With all of these influences acting upon us, one needs to be constantly adjusting to maintain a state of balance in order to interact harmoniously with nature. Also, there are basic attitudes a spiritual student of the Subtle Truth needs to maintain in all circumstances. These are: being an expression of the divine, one conducts oneself with virtue and dignity; one offers oneself selflessly and unconditionally to the world; all actions are spontaneous, and arise from the universal self; one always tries to respond appropriately to every situation; one is at ease with oneself and with others and never contends; one lives a simple, unadorned life and never tries to stand out; one maintains a sense of awe and wonderment with life; one's spirit is calm and unattached in all circumstances; one does not hold attitudes, even these.

In addition to these general guidelines, there are specific practices and postures to develop one's subtle energy. The first one we will discuss is that of rising early. Since the most beneficial time of day is from three to seven a.m., that is the best time for cultivation. By sitting up in a certain position, the body is like an antenna receiving energy. These early morning hours are very good for quiet sitting, while sunrise is best for Eight Treasures, *T'ai Chi*, or some other form of active cultivation.

Just before and just after sunrise is the best time to absorb the energy from the sun. This is done by facing the sun and inhaling the rays into the mouth and then swallowing them down into your lower center. Do this in three series of three. When inhaling, both nostrils should be fully open and in use. During the daytime it is important to know which nostril you are breathing through at any given time in order to reach awareness. If you find that your breathing is constantly shifting from one nostril to the other, it is a sign that you are having a hard time maintaining a balance of *yin* and *yang*. The natural balance is when you breathe through the right (*yin*) nostril from 5 p.m. to 3 a.m., and through the left (*yang*) nostril from 3 a.m. to 5 p.m. There are special guidances in which one or the other nostril is used for the purpose of balance or bringing good fortune.

Another practice that can be carried out anytime during the day is to keep the tongue curled and in contact with the roof of the mouth when you are not using it. This acts as a bridge between the two major energy channels of the body and helps keep the energy from flowing out of the head. This is especially helpful to people whose energy tends to accumulate in their heads and and then dissipate through excessive thinking, talking and general restlessness.

Fundamental Hand Position

Our hands embody all the energy of the universe and can be used to help us harmonize with universal energies. The twelve earthly energies are manifested in the hand as shown in Figure 5. Because Wu is associated with Noon, the *yang* time of the day, and Tzu is associated with Midnight, the *yin* time of day, connecting these two together brings the height of *yin* and *yang* together. This is done by grasping the first knuckle of the ring finger of the left hand with the thumb and middle finger of the right hand. Then join the thumb and middle finger of the left hand so that they encircle the thumb of the right hand (Figure 6). This connects the *yin* point of the left hand with the *yang* point of the right hand. The hands are then held together over the navel (Figure 7). This is a standard sitting cultivation.

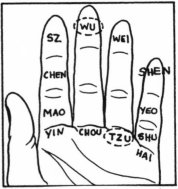

Twelve Earthly Energies
(Figure 5)

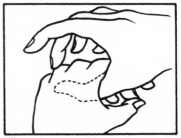

Fundamental Hand Position
(Figure 6)

Greeting

Whenever we approach the Master or the Shrine, we bow while holding our hands in the following position. The thumbs are pressed together (this brings the *yin* and *yang* of the upper body together) while the rest of the fingers curve inward and point straight into the body. The hands are held in front of the energy center of the heart or the navel (Figure 8). The fingers pointing in help focus the energy into these important centers. This hand position can also be used while doing silent sitting or walking cultivation.

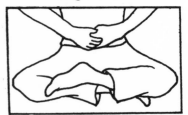

Standard Sitting Cultivation
(Figure 7)

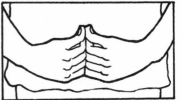

Hand Position for Focusing
(Figure 8)

Salutation

In the Ceremony of Renewal (see page 160) there are many salutations to the spiritual ancestors, and while creating a response from them, the salutations also stimulate one's own energy centers. The salutation is also effective in centering oneself and in draining excess energy out of the head. It is good to do any time you feel uncentered, and especially just before you do silent cultivation. The posture starts in a kneeling position with the right foot over the left foot (Figure 9). This contains the *yang* energy of the left leg. The hands come together over the head so that the middle finger of the right hand (the Tiger Channel) can touch each center. This finger is curved in so that the only part that touches the centers is the knuckle closest to the fingernail. The thumbs come together as before, only now the right hand is inside the left so the knuckle of the middle finger can point down (Figure 10).

First, touch the crown center at the top of the head (Figure 11). Then touch the area between and slightly above the eyebrows (Figure 12). This center is the first of the three Tan Tiens (the Elixir Field, or alchemical center) and is related to the Heavenly Sphere.

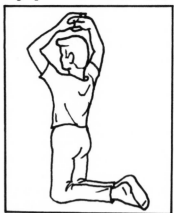

Kneeling Position
(Figure 9)

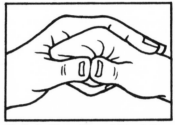

Salutation Hand Position
(Figure 10)

1000 Meeting Point
(Figure 11)

Upper Tan Tien
(Figure 12)

Then touch the area under the nose (Figure 13). This is where the Governing Channel ends. Next touch the throat area (Figure 14) or Adam's Apple. Then touch the heart area (Figure 15). This is the Middle *Tan Tien* or the Human Sphere. Then touch the Lower *Tan Tien* below the navel (Figure 16), the Earthly Sphere. After that, bow down so that the backs of your hands rest on the floor with the middle knuckle pointing up. Rest your head so that the knuckle is touching the Upper *Tan Tien* between the eyebrows (Figure 17). Hold this position for a while and then rise to the kneeling position again and repeat the process in series of threes until you feel calm and centered.

End of Governing Channel
(Figure 13)

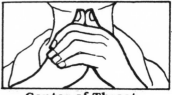

Center of Throat
(Figure 14)

Middle Tan Tien
(Figure 15)

Summoning Creative Yang Energy

As you touch each energy center, invoke the name of the Heavenly General that resides there: Crown Center - *Ja Tsu*; Upper *Tan Tien* - *Ja Shu*; Mouth - *Ja Shen*; Throat - *Ja Wu*; Heart Center - *Ja Chen*; Lower *Tan Tien* - *Ja Ying*.

Lower Tan Tien
(Figure 16)

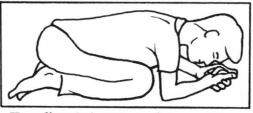

Kneeling Salutation   (Figure 17)

THE FIVE CULTIVATIONS
Introduction

Whether you are sitting, standing, walking, sleeping or doing movement in any way, you can be in a state of cultivation, as long as your attitude is one of relaxed attentiveness. This attitude makes it possible to experience every moment as eternity. With thinking calmed, it is much easier to realize the already existent state of non-dual awareness.

In the old days, a person would devote a lifetime to only one practice, but since modern students like to know everything and do nothing, I offer the following fundamental methods of cultivation in the hope that you will find one you like and stick with it until you truly achieve something.

Sitting Cultivation

Sitting cultivation may be done in either of two positions, sitting on the heels (Figure 18) or in a cross-legged position (Figure 19). Both positions require a thick mat or cushion to relieve pressure on the legs. If you sit on the heels, place the right foot over the left, as in doing the salutation. If you sit cross-legged, be sure the left leg is on top. The hands are in the position called "Harmony" (palms face up, one palm cupping the other, thumbs pointing straight up with tips together). Be sure the spine is straight but relaxed. Unlike other methods, the head is tilted downward slightly. This, along with the tongue being curled, facilitates the flow of energy down out of the head. Eyes should be half-closed and attention focused on breathing until you feel centered. If you are celibate, keep your eyes open; otherwise the sexual energy is too stimulating. Keep the mind centered and do not anticipate results.

Sitting Cultivation on Heels
(Figure 18)

Sitting Cultivation Crosslegged
(Figure 19)

Standing Cultivation - Men

Place the feet shoulder width apart with feet slightly pigeon-toed. The knees are bent and buttocks are tucked in to straighten the spine (Figure 20). The arms make a circle in front of the body, with the elbows raised and fingertips a few inches apart. The shoulders are slightly rounded, and again, the head is tilted downward and the tongue is curled.

In this position, experience yourself as the wick of a lantern. From the great reservoir of energies of the Earth, the life force rises unimpeded from the bottom of your feet up to the top of your head.

Standing Cultivation for Men
(Figure 20)

Standing Cultivation - Women

This position is held with the right foot positioned in front of the left foot so that the big toe of the left foot is touching the heel of the right foot which is on a diagonal to the left foot (Figure 21). The hands are held at the middle *Tan Tien* in the fundamental hand position. Also, the buttocks and stomach are tucked in, the head tilted downward and the tongue curled.

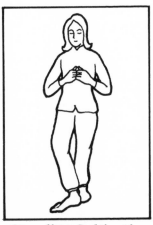

Standing Cultivation for Women
(Figure 21)

Standing Cultivation for Celibate Men

Stand with the feet shoulder width apart and the hands raised over the head in such a way that the palms are turned toward the Heavens with the fingertips pointing toward each other (Figure 22). Look straight ahead unless disturbed by sexual thoughts. In such case, look upward between your hands.

(Figure 22)

Standing Cultivation for Celibate Women

Stand with the feet in the same position as the regular standing cultivation for women, but raise the hands over the head so that the fingers point upward and only the fingertips touch. Open the hands as if holding a ball. The shoulders should be comfortably relaxed (Figure 23).

(Figure 23)

Standing Cultivation as a Self-Protection

Stand with the feet in the same position as the women's standing cultivation. Cross the arms at the wrist, with the right arm closest to the body (in practicing *Kung Fu*, the left arm is held closest to the body). Palms face to the side, fingers pointing upward (Figure 24).

(Figure 24)

Sleeping Cultivation

Always be in bed before 10:00 p.m. and, if possible, sit up at 3:00 a.m. until rising at sunrise in the cool months, or two to three hours before sunrise in the hot months. Before falling asleep, lie on one side or the other (not on the back or the front) and tuck the top leg up, while keeping the other leg straight. The hand on the underside of the body supports the head in such a way that the hand encircles the ear with the thumb resting behind the ear while the palm rests over the temple. The upper arm can rest either on the side or be folded so that the closed fist rests over the navel (Figure 25). This position helps prevent nightmares or sexual stimulation in dreams. Also see Figure 32.

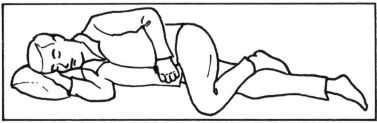

Sleeping Cultivation   (Figure 25)

Walking Cultivation - Slow

This cultivation is done slowly and evenly. The hands are in the fundamental position in front of the lower *Tan Tien*. Focusing on the ground directly in front of you, the steps are done as slowly as possible without losing your balance. Step on the heel of the foot first, and slowly roll onto the toes while bringing the foot in the rear forward at the same speed that everything else is done. Many students have trouble keeping the speed of both feet consistent. Repeating a verse is helpful in focusing the mind while practicing walking cultivation.

Walking Cultivation - Fast

By simply holding your thumbs in your fists and focusing your mind, you can turn an ordinary walk into a cultivation. The thumb must lie on top of the Heaven line in the palm (the head line in Western palmistry). Focus directly in front of you and let the arms swing freely. If your *yang* energy is low, swing the left arm vigorously while restraining the right arm. This will increase the *yang* energy in the body.

Examples of Guiding Verses While Doing Walking Cultivation

These can be recited while you are walking with high concentration.

I

Empty-handed, I am holding a bowl.
Walking on foot, I am riding a buffalo.
Crossing a bridge, I don't see the water,
But the bridge flows!

II

I inquired of a boy under an old pine tree,
"My Master is gathering herbs," he said.
"He's on the mountain amidst the clouds,
I know not where."

III

The prince searched for the
Master in the high mountains.
He stayed in his cave for seven days.
He was taught to make immortal medicine.
When he returned to the world,
A thousand years had passed.

IV

A Master said to his disciples,
"If I meet a man with a cane,
I will take it away.
If I meet a man without a cane,
I will give him mine."
Isn't he a tricky old fellow!

Moving Cultivation

Although all movement can be a cultivation, probably the most perfect expression of the rhythm and power of nature is the practice of *Tai Chi* movement and its prerequisite, the Eight Treasures. Many good books on this subject have already been written, so it is only necessary to mention that there are three styles in this tradition which express natural spiritual principles. They are all interrelated and are called Gentle Path, Sky Journey, and Infinite Expansion styles. The popular *Yang* Style is close to the Gentle Path style, or Style of Harmony, which relates to the Lower *Tan Tien*. The *Chen* Style is close to the Sky Journey or Style of Naturalness, which relates to the Middle *Tan Tien*. There is no popular style which corresponds to the Infinite Expansion Style or Style of Integration, which relates to the Upper *Tan Tien* and brings all three *Tan Tiens* together.

All students should learn the Eight Treasures first, however, because many people have serious energy blocks and the Eight Treasures is more effective in quickly breaking through them than the more subtle *Tai Chi*.

Tai Chi movement has a slight suggestion of the martial arts or fighting skills, but this is only a side effect. It is not the direct expression of peaceful spiritual cultivation. The main difference between *Tai Chi* movement and the martial arts is that the martial arts were designed for fighting, while body movement for spiritual cultivation is based on the principles of energy guidance.

The term *Kung Fu*, if narrowly used, designates a martial art. In its broad sense, however, it represents the formula: method + time + practice = achievement. Thus, any artistic achievement and special skill can be called a *Kung Fu*. Cultivation requires constant practice, yet external practice cannot be recognized as enlightenment; it is merely a way to help you reach enlightenment.

Everyone has one side of the body that is stronger than the other; usually this is the right side. The learning and practice of a martial art usually leads the imbalance to an extreme, like other sports and games. Since the purpose of *Tai Chi* is primarily the correction of imbalance, correct practice will involve both sides of the body. Thus, one should not only do the habitual right-sided *T'ai Chi* movements, but also include the corresponding left-sided movements as well. Also, the upper and lower parts of the body need to harmonize.

In general, all disease is only a partial problem. Even if it is a weakness of the entire nervous system, it is still only partial. It is partial because there are two other spheres of life: mind and spirit. *T'ai Chi* is aimed at the harmony and restoration of all three. In the *Tao Teh Ching* this is called "reaching gentleness as the major trait of life." It is also the integration of inner and outer being.

AUXILIARY PRACTICES
(Note: The Purifications on pages 92-95 should be completed before beginning any of the circulatory practices.)

The Internal Movement of Chi
Chi circulates continuously through all the channels in the body, and the flow of *chi* can be strengthened by mental conductance. Most people's *chi* is weak or stagnant, usually in cavities where the channels are more narrow or harder to penetrate. The purpose of circulating *chi* is to open areas of blockage and enable the *chi* to flow smoothly.

The front, *yin* channel, which is called the Conception or Bearing Channel (*Ren Mei*), has a negative polarity. The *yang* channel on the back, which is called the Governing Channel (*Du Mei*), has a positive polarity. When the *chi* of these two channels is flowing smoothly, all is well, so keeping them unblocked and clear is basic to all other practices.

The Bearing Channel originates at the perineum (Sea Bottom Cavity) which is also called *Yin* Intersection in acupuncture. It ascends along the interior of the abdomen along the front midline to the throat and then curves around the lips, passes through the cheek and enters the infraorbital region (under the eyes). In cultivation, *chi* flows from the head to the perineum.

The Governing Channel also originates at the perineum but ascends up through the spinal column to DU 16 (directly below the external occipital protuberance) where it enters the brain. It then ascends to the crown of the head and winds down the forehead to the roots of the upper teeth.

These two channels are not connected at the top. When the tongue touches the roof of the mouth, the *yin* and *yang* channels are connected and the circuit is complete. We frequently touch the roof of our mouth with the tongue during everyday activities; however, in meditation, a continuous circuit is important. The tongue should be relaxed; if it is tense, it can result in stagnation of the *chi.* The tongue should not touch the teeth or the connection will not be effective, and one tends to become sleepy. The tongue also should not be stretched back too far or it will be tight and the *chi* will stagnate. The spot on the soft palate where the tongue touches is called Heaven's Pond (*Tien Tzie*) or Dragon Spring (*Lung Chuan*).

The Three Tan Tiens

The human body is divided into three major areas. Each area has three *yang* energy centers on the Governor Channel, and three *yin* centers on the Conception Channel. Thus, there are nine *yang* centers running up the back, and nine *yin* centers running down the front (see Figure 26).

The middle center of each section is the most important and is called a *Tan Tien* or "Field of Elixir" (*Qihai*, Sea of Chi). Each *Tan Tien* is also associated with a specific gland.

The head area is considered the Heavenly Realm. The Upper *Tan Tien* is located between the eyebrows and is associated with the pineal gland, which is in the center of the head.

The upper trunk, including the throat and chest, is considered the Human Realm. The Middle *Tan Tien* is located between the nipples and is associated with the thymus.

The lower trunk or torso is considered the Earth Realm. The Lower *Tan Tien*, located approximately 1.5 inches below the navel, is associated with the prostate or ovaries. This *Tan Tien* is also called The Furnace or *For Lu.*

The Great Outer Circulation

The Great Outer Circulation enhances one's energy flow by encouraging the movement of energy in a circle through the *Ren* and the *Du* channels. The Great Outer Circulation should be done in a sitting meditation posture so that the *chi* does not sink down into the legs. If allowed to travel downward, it could stagnate in some of the leg cavities. This could later affect the leg's circulation and cause problems.

Guidelines for Practice:
* Sit either cross-legged or on the heels.
* Use a mat or cushion to relieve pressure on the legs.
* When sitting on the heels, place the right foot over the left. If you sit cross-legged, be sure the left leg is on top.
* Keep the spine straight but relaxed.
* Tilt the head down slightly to help energy flow out of the head.
* Touch the tongue to the roof of the mouth.
* Mentally touch the centers as you inhale up the spine and exhale down the front of the body.
* Keep a relaxed, flexible attitude.
* Do not be forceful or anticipate results.
* Let the mind guide the *chi* consciously throughout its circulation. Keep the mind on the next cavity and let the *chi* get there by itself.

Energy Centers of the Great Outer Circulation

The *chi* passes through other points along the way; however, the nine major points of the front and back should be used to help the flow.

Three major cavities, called the Three Gates (*San Guan*), offer the greatest resistance. The first, *Wei Lu*, is located on the tailbone. Here the bone structure narrows the channel and after the teen years, the sacral vertebrae fuse. *Wei Lu* offers the most resistance.

The next major obstacle is *Ling Tai* (Spiritual Tower). It is located between thoracic vertebra 6 and 7. If the *chi* remains in this area, it can disturb the heart. Usually the best way to eliminate resistance here is to relax.

Yu Gen (Jade Pillow) is located at the base of the skull, at the external occipital protuberance. The channel is constricted here because of the skull structure. If the *chi* does not flow easily here, it may pass into other channels in the head and cause headaches.

Circulate the energy through the points listed below and illustrated in Figure 26. Although at first the feeling will be mostly imaginary, perseverance will bring more perceptible results. Since *chi* follows the mind, keeping your attention from point to point will create a stronger flow and gradually open the constrictions.

When circulating *chi* up the back, one may feel slight muscular tension and warming as the *chi* passes. However, only a tingling sensation will be felt on the head, because the muscle layer is very thin.

Yang Centers

#1 Perineum

#2 On the lower sacral vertebra, *Wei Lu*, opposite the Lower *Tan Tien*

#3 On the spine between the spinous processes of the second and third lumbar vertebra (slightly above the navel) *Ming Min - Du 4*

#4 On the spine between the spinous processes of the ninth and tenth thoracic vertebra (half-way between points 3 and 5) - *Du 8*

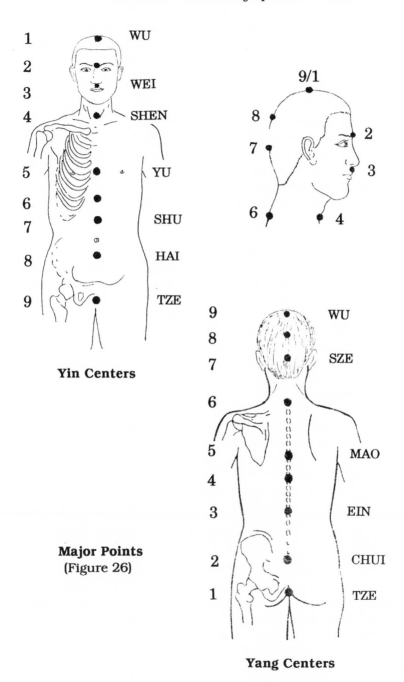

Yin Centers

1	WU
2	
3	WEI
4	SHEN
5	YU
6	
7	SHU
8	HAI
9	TZE

Major Points
(Figure 26)

9/1

8

7

2

3

6

4

Yang Centers

9	WU
8	
7	SZE
6	
5	MAO
4	
3	EIN
2	CHUI
1	TZE

#5 On the spine between thoracic vertebra 6 and 7 (opposite the heart center) *Lingtai - Du 10* (The number 5 always denotes the center of something.)

#6 On the spine at the bone protuberance at the base of the neck (cervical vertebra 7) *Du 14*

#7 Base of the skull at the external occipital protuberance (opposite the base of the nose) "Jade Pillow Point"

#8 Center of the back of the head at the point where the parietal bones and occipital bone meet, opposite the Upper *Tan Tien*

#9 Crown of the head, *Baihui - Du 20*

Yin Centers

#1 Crown of the head - Baihui-Du 20

#2 Upper Tan Tien (between the eyebrows)

#3 Base of the nose

#4 Base of the neck (just below Adam's apple)

#5 Middle Tan Tien (between the nipples) - Ren 17

#6 Bottom of the sternum (xiphoid process)

#7 A few inches above the navel.

#8 Lower Tan Tien (approximately 1.5 inches below the navel)

#9 Perineum

Major and Minor Orbit Circulation

Minor Orbit Circulation just circulates your energy around the mid-line of the body, in the back and front, whereas Major Orbit Circulation includes both legs. In Major Orbit Circulation, when your energy reaches the perineum, conduct the energy down the inside of the legs all the way to the point in the center of the sole of the feet (Rushing Fountain, Kidney-1). Then follow the outside of the leg, bringing the energy back to the tailbone, then all the way up to complete the Minor Orbit Circulation. Usually the Lower *Tan Tien* is the starting and termination point. The Lower Tan Tien is recommended for elderly or weaker people; for healthy younger people, it is proper to use the Middle *Tan Tien.*

Minor Orbit Circulation is a basic method for the self-conduction of internal energy. It can prepare you for soul travel, but it is not an isolated achievement. All practices and learning are important, because there are many levels in the overall achievement leading to immortality.

More information about the checkpoints and other disciplines can be found in my work *The Esoteric Tao Teh Ching*. Minor Orbit Circulation is a good foundation for both physical and spiritual health.

Minor Orbit Circulation is usually done seated in a cross-legged position. Major Orbit Circulation is done sitting on a chair or in a standing position. When the *chi* goes through the legs, a feeling of warmth often surges through the energy channel.

Regarding the checkpoints in the Minor Orbit Circulation: in the beginning you s hould use the mind to conduct the *chi*, especially at the time of night when your energy is naturally concentrated in the sexual center. In this way you can that pressure away. You can alleviate congestion in this area by making circles with the eyes 36 times, but with the eyelids closed. This helps pull the congested energy up to the head so that it can continue to circulate.

When a real breakthrough occurs, there is a kind of shock or strong vibration or internal noise. One who does quiet sitting daily makes the openness of each checkpoint on the front and back their goal, especially for the back. The opening of each checkpoint is a spiritual achievement. When all the checkpoints on the front and back open up, you will not be sick any more. This is achieved by constant practice. Such achievement is usually the testimony of people in their middle age, but many young people also mention having such experiences. Realistically speaking, it seems that health is achieved by many years of constant daily spiritual cultivation that builds up a strong electrical current that can prevent all possible physical problems.

Minor Orbit Circulation is traditionally recommended because the spinal cord definitely plays a role in health by connecting all the different organs and the nervous system. Major Orbit Circulation was a later addition of teachers with and interest in martial arts.

There is still another method called 36 Orbit Circulation. This was developed for profound martial arts purposes. The number 36 means 36 grades or positions of the physical body. Thirty-six important points of the body are used for moving your energy. There are hundreds of energy-moving patterns created by different people, but the basic pattern is still the fundamental practice of the Minor Orbit Circulation. Even the practices which circulate energy into the major organs are not as important as bringing energy to the spine so that it strengthens the whole nervous system and reaches everywhere in the body.

One can ignore the Minor Orbit Circulation if one is functioning naturally. The most useful cultivation is to concentrate on the spine as the source of great benefit. This has been hinted at by Chuang Tzu.

The fourth generation of Master Chen Tuan's students who achieved greatness in *I Ching* practice were highly respected. Master Sou Yung described the importance of the meeting or alignment of one's energy at two points: the Thousand Meeting Point on the top of the head (also called the Mud Pill), and the center of the lower abdomen, which includes the tailbone and perineum. Then the energy spreads warmth throughout the whole body. His poem is as follows:

> *The thirty-six palaces all return to be Spring*
> *when the Heavenly Root meets the Home of Moon.*

Thirty-six palaces refers to thirty-six areas of the whole body. Surely it does not bring the result that martial arts people expect, which is external fighting strength. The achievement is the enduring life force. This is truly a useful practice.

Gathering the Heavenly Energies

There are ten Heavenly Stems (energies), five *yin* and five *yang*. The *yang* stems are *Jia, Bien, Wuh, Geng, and Ren*. The *yin* stems are *Yi, Ding, Ji, Hsin, and Quei*. While in one of the sitting positions, pull these energies down (from Heaven) into the center of the head, down the center of the body and into the lower trunk. Men should concentrate on the five *yin* energies, and women should concentrate on the five *yang* energies. Each energy relates to a different area of the body. Imagine *Jia/Yi* energy flowing into the throat area, *Bien/Ding* energy into the head, *Wuh/Ji* energy into the stomach, *Geng/Hsin* energy into the upper chest, and *Ren/Quei* energy into the lower trunk (Figure 27). Keep in mind that this gathering is internal, whereas the Great Circulation is close to the surface of the skin.

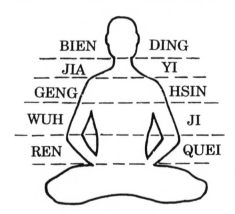

The Natural Energies of Life
(Figure 27)

Fire energy *(Bien/Ding)* is the energy of the mind. Wood energy *(Jia/Yi)*, is the energy of the nerves. Metal energy *(Geng/Hsin)* is the energy of the respiratory system. Earth energy *(Wuh/Ji)* is the energy of the digestive system. Water energy *(Ren/Quei)* is the energy of the reproductive system.

Opening Up the Three Tan Tien

This is one of the major exercises in self-cultivation. While in a sitting position, you may want to open up the three major energy centers. This is done by visualizing the following three characters superimposed over each center: *Jia*, 甲 over the Upper *Tan Tien*; *Shen*, 申 , over the Middle *Tan Tien*; and *Yeo*, 由 over the Lower *Tan Tien* (Figure 28). Touch each center with the hands in the salutation position while repeating the sound of each character. *Jia* is fairly high pitched, *Shen* is mid-ranged and *Yeo* is lower on the scale. Repeat these in a series of three as you guide your energy to awaken these three centers.

Three Tan Tien
(Figure 28)

Opening the Six Jia Centers

While doing any of the salutations, ceremonies or invocations which invoke the creative *yang* energy, you may want to open and clear out these centers. Trace the character *Jia*, 甲 (as shown in Figure 30) with your right middle finger over the same six centers you touch in the salutation (Figure 29).

Six Jia Centers
(Figure 29)

Untying the Spirits

Find a dimly lit place in the evening, preferably after the evening meal. Sit upright in a chair with the left thumb held in the fist. The right hand then traces the same character, *Jia*, over the chest. In this exercise, all the fingers of the right hand come together like the beak of a bird. Start at the right nipple and trace a big circle up over the chest and down through the left nipple and down around the stomach and up to the right nipple again. Repeat this two times. Then move your hand up near the throat area and straight down to the Lower *Tan Tien* (Figure 30). Repeat in a series of three. As you do this you may yawn a lot or experience a tingling sensation in your mouth and taste sweet saliva.

Untying the Spirits
(Figure 30)

These experiences are not the goal, just signs that you are on the right track, so do not take them too seriously.

Untying the spirits is for the preparation of the independence of the immortal soul. Souls have an invisible connection to physical life that becomes a bondage. True spiritual freedom depends on integrating the souls and cutting their dependence on and tight connection with one's physical body.

Purifying Bad Energy

The *T'ai Chi Tu* 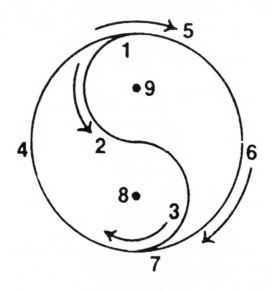 is a powerful symbol, especially if drawn by someone of power and balance. For instance, if you are served food that you are suspicious of and do not want to return it, just draw this symbol over it in the air and it will purify any bad energy that may be around. Use the middle finger of the right hand to trace the outline as shown in Figure 31.

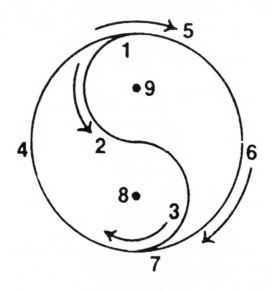

T'ai Chi Tu
(Figure 31)

Make points 8 and 9 as if you were dotting the letter "i". It is also a safe practice to make the symbol over your car before driving somewhere. If you are sufficiently cultivated, you can even subdue an attacker with it. So remember, if any situation has bad or excessive energy, this symbol will tend to purify it.

Warding off Possible Trouble

Whenever you get a strong feeling that something bad is about to happen, or if your body signals that something ominous is in the air (for instance, a strong eye twitch for no apparent reason is sometimes a signal that something bad is about to happen), then face the East, inhale deeply through the nose, bite your teeth together three times and turn to the West and exhale through your mouth. Repeat this three times.

Revitalizing Your Energy

When you are tired and need some quick energy, lie in a semi-reclining position facing East, with your legs out straight. Place the right foot over the left. Hold the thumbs inside the fists and place the fists over the two energy centers of the chest. The right fist should be over the heart center, and the left over the lower Tan Tien (Figure 32). You may even sleep in this position. Hold it until your energy is back to normal.

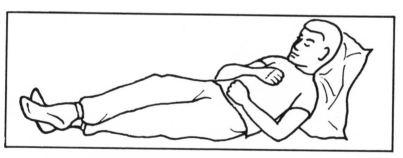

Revitalizing Your Energy
(Figure 32)

Draining Off Anger

If you cannot seem to get rid of anger over a particular situation, sit in a chair and clasp your hands together in such a way that the fingers interlock from the opposite direction than they normally would (Figure 33). It is done by placing the left hand near your right shoulder and the right hand near the left. Then slide them together with the palms facing each other until you can interlock the fingers together. Then pull your interlocked hands down the center of your chest, forcing the elbows away from the body until your arms are totally extended and the hands are pointing down (Figure 34). Your hands should be over the lower *Tan Tien.*

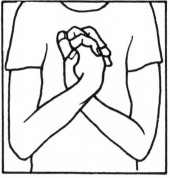

(Figure 33)

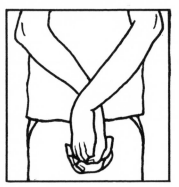

(Figure 34)

First Aid to a Spiritually Troubled Person

It might happen that someone in your surroundings becomes possessed by a spirit or suffers temporary mental loss. In these cases, you can use your left hand to hold their head, while using the thumb and index finger of your right hand to pinch the flesh between the nostrils (Figure 35). This makes the person feel pain and helps restore normal consciousness. If, however, they are extremely disturbed and you wish to have protection for yourself as you aid them, draw the character for Heaven, 天 in the palm of

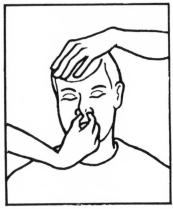

(Figure 35)

your left hand with the middle finger of the right hand. Then wrap the fingers of your left hand around the thumb to make a fist.

For your own personal protection, use your thumb and the forefinger of your left hand to lightly pinch the partition between your nostrils. Do this twenty-one times and then press the inner corners of both eyes. Do this every morning after rising and it should keep you safe spiritually.

Conclusion

The postures and practices introduced in this book are presented with specific details. In real practice, however, there are variations to these according to the age and level of development of the student, time of the year, social and environmental considerations, etc. For someone who is truly developed, the significance, value and details of these practices will be spontaneously understood. For most, having personal guidance is still the best way to proceed because a truly achieved teacher can always recognize your level and know how to best direct your growth.

My intention is to offer these basic esoteric practices now so there will be no delay in improving yourself. Be aware that these practices are only one aspect of your spiritual development. To assure your successful achievement you must also work earnestly to improve the virtuous quality of your life.

The Red Baby

Q: In Chapter 55 of the Tao Teh Ching it says, "The one who maintains the highest integrity is as a newborn baby. Poisonous insects do not bite it, fierce animals do not attack it. Predatory birds do not seize it. Its bones are weak, its tendons are soft and its hold is tight. Its member stirs without knowing sex. This expresses the fullness of its vitality. It does not become hoarse with crying all day. This expresses its harmony."

I understand and accept most of that chapter, but I do not understand the part about the insects and animals and birds not attacking the baby.   Do those sentences have some particular spiritual meaning?

Master Ni: Yes, they are connected with a great spiritual secret which was explained in metaphor by an open-minded and responsible Master named Kou Hong in his invaluable work, the *Pau Po Tzu*. His book deals with a pivotal point in the pursuit of divine immortality. The image of the new born baby is that of a nude baby with wings. Here is the story.

"The 'new born baby,' in Chinese, is also called the 'Red Baby.' It is also designated as the 'True One.' In the Immortal Tradition, it is the spiritual being which is conceived as the result of cultivation. The Red Baby is the result of a mystical pregnancy and the birth of the highest divine being which embodies Tao.

"The Red Baby is a perfect being who needs neither food nor clothing and who lives harmoniously and transcendently within the universe. The Red Baby is a completely super-natural being, and since it is the completion of human spiritual life, it can travel to the stars or anywhere in space. Its virtuous nature never fades, and pain never overtakes it.

"As humans became corrupt and competitive, their intellectual minds became dualistic, thus they strayed from and lost their true nature. Only a few humans can now achieve the mystical pregnancy and birth, the mystical metamorphosis of the Red Baby. From those of dualistic mind, the Red Baby can never be born.

"All of us, as human beings, accumulate earthly habits and attachments which become obstacles to conceiving and nurturing the Red Baby. Not all people can give birth to Red Babies because the Red Baby is the highest true spiritual upliftment possible from our crude level of being."

Q: Can you teach us how to cultivate and attain it?

Master Ni: That is a question of great weight. There are strong prohibitions protecting high spiritual secrets from the unrefined majority. I will translate a chapter of the *Pau Po Tzu* for you which may answer some of your questions about this. You must understand that Master Kou Hong was risking his own spiritual exposure to the Heavenly prohibitions, so he wrote it in metaphor. As a student of the same spiritual tradition, I respect the seriousness of the matter and his limitations are also mine. However, all of us can benefit from Master Kou's legacy. With that in mind, I present the chapter called "The True One."

"In ancient times there were those who attained to the True One, yet maintained what they really were. Heaven attained the True One and became pure. Earth attained the True One and became stable. All spirits attained the True One and became vitalized. Virtuous rulers attained the True One and became the power of righteousness.

"If Heaven were to lose the True One, it would lose its purity and unity and become split. If Earth were to lose the True One, it would lose its stability and become barren. If all spirits were to lose the True One, they would lose their responsiveness and perish. If the Valley of the Universe were to lose the True One, it would lose its productiveness and become exhausted. If all lives were to lose the True One, they would lose their vitality and be extinguished. If rulers were to lose the True One they would lose their righteousness and decline."

What is the True One in the cultivation of the Integral Way? Philosophically speaking it means "oneness" or "unity." On the spiritual level, the *Pau Po Tzu* elucidates as follows,

> *"I once heard my teacher say,*
> *'If people could know the True Divine One,*
> *then they would have accomplished all*
> *learning in life.'"*
> (Chapter 19, Spirits on Earth)

"If one could know the True One, there would be nothing left unknown. If one does not know the True One, he truly knows nothing. The Integral Way of the universe starts from the honored True One and develops into the three realms of Heaven, Earth and Man. Heaven received the True One and became pure; Earth received the True One and became tranquil; Man received the True One and became vitalized; the Gods received the True One and became powerful.

"Metal sinks, feathers float, mountains loom and rivers flow. All things find their own true nature. However, eyes cannot see the True One, nor can ears hear it. Things remain in existence as long as they are preserved with the True One, and they perish when the True One is neglected. When facing the True One, good fortune appears and when one turns one's back on the True One, misfortune occurs. While the True One is maintained, prosperity is endless. If the True One is neglected, breath is exhausted and life ceases. The lord of old says, 'The image of the True One is elusive and evasive.' The classics of divine immortality say, 'If you wish to be immortal, you must embrace the True One. When you are hungry, keep thinking of the True One and you shall obtain food. When you are thirsty, keep thinking of the True One, and you shall obtain drink.'

"In spiritual practice, the True One (internal spirits) also possesses names, with certain uniforms and in colors as the subtle shape. In the male it is 0.9 inches long (in subtle measurement), and in the female it is 0.6 subtle inches. Sometimes it is located three inches below the navel, which is the Lower Field of Immortal cultivation. At other times it is located in the Golden Gate or Purple Palace, one inch behind the space between one's eyebrows, which forms the Hall of Illumination. Two inches inside the Purple Palace, the Upper Field of Immortal Cultivation is formed.

"The True One can give life to *yin* and beget *yang*; bring on cold or heat. From the True One there is sprouting in spring, growing in summer, harvesting in autumn and storing in winter. All space is not enough for its magnitude. Yet neither a hair nor a sprout is tiny enough to express its minuteness.

"Of old, when passing Mount Wind on the road east to Mount Green, the Yellow Emperor met the Master of the Purple Palace and received from him the *Sacred Book of the Inner Secret of the Three Divinities*, which enabled him to summon and direct all divinities. On going south to Shady Tree, on the northern slope of Round Knoll, he surveyed the place mounted by the spirits, gathered mystical flowers of *yang* energy and drank from the stream of Red Knoll. In the west he met Master Chung Kua Tzu and received *The Classic of Self-Completion* from Master Kuang Chen Tzu. On the way north to Hung Bank he mounted Chu Tzu and met the Lord of Ta Wei and the ever-youthful Huang Kai from whom he received the 'Drawings of Mystical Mushrooms.' While returning to his duties as emperor he obtained 'The Golden Secret of the Immortal Medicine.'

"On Mount O-Mei he met Tien Che, the God-man, in the Jade Chamber, and inquired of him concerning the process of the way of the True One. His reply was, 'Since you are already the great sovereign over the world, isn't it avarice on your part to seek divine immortality?'

"It is impossible to give their conversation in full, but one aspect of it was this, 'As for the formula leading to spiritual immortality and godhead, there is only "gold" and "cinnabar"; for the preservation of eternal life and dissolving evils, there is only the way of embracing the True One.'

"The ancient classics of divine immortality say that 'the Nine-Time Recycling Immortal Medicine,' the 'Golden Liquid Classic,' and the 'Secret Instructions for Embracing the True One' are stored in a jade box from the spiritual five cities of Mount Kun Lun; that they are engraved on golden plaques sealed with purple; and that they bear the imprint of the seal of states. I learned the instructions from my teacher in this way.

"The True One is North in the Grand Abyss, up front in the Chamber of Illumination (between the eyebrows), at the rear in the Purple Palace. Its flowered umbrella (eyebrows) is near the gold Pavilion. To the left and right are the stars of the Big Dipper. It is like a dashing wave in the void. It is the dark projection on steep ledges, the vermillion grass in the thickets, the white jade in the high mountains, the sun and the moon shedding their light. The True One passes through fire and water, traverses Heaven, and fords Earth. Its cities and castles intertwine; its tents and canopies are studded with gems. Lines of dragons and tigers guard the True One; gods stand at its side. Neither retaining nor dispensing, the True One enjoys peace wherever it is.

Neither dilatory nor rushing, the True One enjoys security in its abode. Able to take both ease and precaution, the True One never quits.

"Embrace the One and guard the True, then you can communicate with the gods. Lessen desires, restrain from eating too much, and the True One will abide quietly.

"Even when the sharp blade is at the base of the throat, we shall live as if embracing the True One.

"The True One is not hard to know; lack of persistence is the difficulty. Guard it without losing it and you will never reach exhaustion. On land it meets no evil animals; in water it dispels crocodiles and dragons. It fears neither demons nor poisonous insects. Ghosts dare not approach it, nor blades strike it. This is the basic knowledge of the True One."

Kou Hong continues, "My own teacher, Master Cheng the hermit, taught me the old spiritual classic of evoking or recalling several thousand methods and procedures for dispelling evils and defending oneself. For example, there were methods for making shadows and the body invisible; methods for suspending one's personal animation; methods for undergoing nine transmutations, twelve transformations and twenty-four births; methods for feeling that one is seeing the gods within one's body and causing them to become visible. All of these were effective. Nevertheless, at times the thought of bringing into existence several thousand spiritual creatures to protect oneself could be so cumbersome that it labors the mind. He felt that if a single process for embracing the True One were known, all these other methods could be less important. This is why the tradition states, 'To know only the One saves you from having to learn multiple methods.'"

(Note: This is the spirit of the simple truth which Lao Tzu represents. The Tao Teh Ching is the culmination of his many years of learning and cultivation. It was not the beginning of ancient natural spiritual teaching.)

"There are clear-cut prerequisites for receiving the secret oral instructions concerning the True One. The lips are smeared with the blood of a white bird. The instructions are received on a propitious day. An agreement is entered into by means of white gauze and white silver. A tally of gold is notched and split. If one expounds these oral instructions lightheartedly or transmits them heedlessly, the gods will not cooperate.

"If a person can embrace the True One, then the True One also embraces that person. In this way, the blade finds no place on one's body for its sharp edge to penetrate; harmful things find no place that will allow entrance. Therefore, in defeat, it is possible to be victorious; in positions of peril it is possible to regain security. Whether in a nest of ghosts, on a mountain of demons, in places suffering plague, in places inhabited by tigers and wolves, in the habitat of snakes, or within a tomb, all evil will go far away as long as one remains diligent in embracing the True One.

"If, on the other hand, you forget to embrace the True One even for a moment, evil ghosts can harm you. If you are lying down and have a nightmare, leave the room quickly and look up to the star of Help in the Big Dipper. Devote yourself firmly to embracing the True One, and evil ghosts will depart immediately. If the weather is rainy, remain in your room, face north and visualize the Star of Help. If you are surrounded by armed bandits and have no refuge, enter immediately into the practice of the Six *Jia* Deities. Protect yourself and embrace the One, and no harm will come to you.

"Anyone who can embrace the True One will be able to travel thousands of miles, enter dangerous territories, and ford large rivers, all without the need of divination for the right day and hour. When beginning a task, or moving to a new home, one will never again depend upon the subtle energy rotation calendar, nor will one need to observe the taboos of Jupiter, the moon, nor even the gods of death. Life's taboos will never again be considered fatal. This is an effective method that has been successfully used by our achieved predecessors.

"The body of an individual can be protected in the same way as a state. The diaphragm may be compared to the palace; the arms and legs to the suburbs and frontiers; the bones and joints to the officials; the heart to the sovereign;

the blood to the ministers; the breath to the population. Therefore, anyone who is able to regulate his own body can regulate a state. To take good care of the population is the best way to make the state secure, and by the same token, to nurture breath is the way to keep the body whole. When the population scatters, a state is ruined. When the breath is exhausted, the body dies. Anything that is dying cannot be living, and anything perishing cannot be in a state of preservation. Therefore, humans in their highest form dissipate fears before they arise and control illness before it occurs. They do not pursue what has already happened. Just as a population is difficult to nurture but easy to endanger, breath is difficult to purify but easy to soil.

"Therefore, a strong and careful center of power is the way to protect a state. The way to strengthen the blood and breath is to whittle down covetousness. Thereafter, the True One survives and the three spiritual sources and seven systems of physical essence of an individual life are preserved. All harm is dispelled and life is extended."

This is the traditional standpoint of immortal teaching, to serve the people and preserve the body as one united principle. This is where Lao Tzu as well as all ancient developed ones stand.

Chapter 8

The Golden Collection
Of Spiritual Practices, Part III

Ceremonial Readings

Ceremony For the Renewal and Enrichment
of Body, Mind and Spirit

This ceremony is especially suitable for weekly, monthly, or yearly renewal. (See page 131 for the salutation and associated postures.) Begin the dedication to the indivisible realm of Tao with nine strikes of the gong.

* * * * *

To readjust yourself with your true origin, recite these words:

As T'ai Chi divides,
Heaven and Earth are spontaneously manifested.
Clear, light energy
becomes the Heavenly Realms.
Dark, heavy energy
becomes the Earthly Realms.
In a human being,
the energies of Heaven and Earth unite.
We cultivate Tao
in order to evolve
and become spiritually everlasting.
The secret of Tao is transmitted to us
through our divine Teachers,
and through studying the sacred books of Tao.
May the Heavenly Jade Emperor,
the source of all Divine Immortals,
who resides in the Golden Shrine
of the highest Pure Realm,
please accept our dedications.

(Three salutations)

*May all the ancestors whose beings united with Tao
before Fu Shi, the wise leader of the Stone Age,
please accept our dedications.
May all Teachers who achieved themselves in Tao
before the Great Yu, Emperor of the Shah Dynasty,
and all enlightened sages, emperors and individuals
who restored their genuine nature since then,
please accept our dedications.*

(Three salutations)

*May the beneficial energy of Wealth, Health,
Peace, Bliss, and Longevity be with us.
May all Heavenly Immortals,
and all Divine Guardians within and outside
our Shrine respond to our sincerity.
Please accept our dedications.*

(Three salutations)

*May the spiritual energy of Harmony and
the union with kindness
accept our dedication.*

(One salutation)

To refresh yourself with Tao, and live a life of high comprehension, recite these words:

*The creative energy of Heaven
is our paternal source.
The receptive energy of Earth
is our maternal source.
All people are offspring
of the same universal Origin.
Within my own true nature
are the same virtues
that belong to inspired sages.
My sincerity is as great
as the sages of all times.*

I recognize my spiritual practice
with my spiritual family
as an expression of the divine order
and harmony which reappears in my life.
I have love for all people
who are in their "winter" years
and wish them to live enjoyably.
I treat all young ones kindly
and help them to have a good life.
The sick and needy are also
my brothers and sisters,
so I protect and shelter
them under my wings.
I assist the talented
and do not waste my own talents.
If I enjoy a good life
and have many things to give,
as Heavenly virtue displays
its benevolence through me.
If I have little and undergo many difficulties,
it is the Heavenly Realm building me stronger.
Only by realizing my pristine nature
can I fulfill the true significance of life.
To ignore the true significance of life
is to sacrifice my spiritual immortality.
To violate the normalcy of my true personality
is to undermine my natural well-being.
By knowing the principles of change
and always doing my best,
I hope to be in harmony
with the enduring Will of the universe.
I gratefully accept what the Life Giver
brings to me and do not cling to sorrows
or try to run away.
With courage I follow Tao
and obey the subtle universal law.
Rather than lose myself
by seeking the luxuries of worldly life,
I cultivate my positive, spiritual energy
in order to actualize an everlasting life.

*In my life I follow only what is good
    and thus never stray from my true nature.
When I transform,
    my energy returns to the Infinite Source of life.
There is never a question of my existence
    or non-existence, because beingness
    and non-beingness are both aspects
    of my true nature.
I confirm the benevolence of the universe
    with my selfless dedication
    to all beings and non-beings.*

Joyfully recite the following to revitalize yourself:

*From all directions comes
    the true, positive energy
    which brings innumerable blessings.
All disasters are eliminated
    and all miseries vanish.
Spirits of the Pure Origin protect me,
    and the eyes of Heavenly Immortals watch over me.
My life is peaceful and trouble-free
    because I unite my heart and mind
    with the eternal Tao.
The balancing, Universal Will
    and my will become one.
The younger brothers and sisters, sons and daughters
    who learn the natural subtle truth
    follow the Tao and use this tradition
    as their vantage point to unite with
    the divine spiritual beings who guard the Shrine.
With endless salutations,
    your humble descendant
    is bathed in divine energy forever.*

(Three salutations)

Simple But Sublime Marriage Ceremony

Tao is one.
It is the perfect harmony of the universe.
Tao divides itself into Heaven and Earth,
   or yin and yang.
It manifests in men and women
   as subtle yin/yang energies.
Men and women complement each other,
   and each contains an integral part of the other.
As students of the Integral Truth,
   a man and a woman
   build their earthly relationship
   on the refinement of their subtle energies.
They cultivate together
   to reach a state of perfect harmony.
Therefore, their relationship remains untouched
   by the constant changes of earthly life.
They unite their virtue in Tao
   and their union is everlasting.
Their lovers' hearts transform to be rainbows,
   that join each other in perfect harmony.
The golden ribbon on (bridegroom's name) neck
   represents the sun.
The silver ribbon on (the bride's name) neck
   represents the moon.
When the great symbols of yin and yang harmonize,
   all beautiful creations come to earth.
In recognizing one another as husband and wife,
   (bridegroom's name) and (bride's name)
   wholeheartedly join each other to become one.
This beautiful marriage shall be fulfilled
   by the witness of all your friends.
I pronounce you husband and wife,
   and sanctify your marriage
   to become a perfect union in Tao.
This Shrine of the Eternal Breath of Universal Essence
   offers three bells to celebrate
   this beautiful marriage.

Ritual of Mind Ceremony

Since the beginning of time,
  Tao has been manifesting.
It has been transmitted
  for countless generations.
All things receive life from Heaven.
Heaven does not abandon people,
  it is people who turn away from Heaven.
Because of Heaven's love
  one is able to receive
  the correct methods for self-cultivation.
Through Heaven's kindness,
  one is able to melt away
  the vicious qualities of one's old self
  and rebuild kind qualities of a new self
  that becomes more pure with each passing day.
As mental obstacles disappear,
  the heart becomes bright with inner light.
Through diligent cultivation,
  one will be benefitted
  by many subtle spiritual responses
  that reform one's life from the old way
  to a new pure way.
One's chi becomes pure,
  and the heart unites with Oneness.
When our activities are simple and clear,
  life becomes naturally virtuous.
With sincerity and determination,
  one is guided back to the Truth.
The heart reaches out to connect with Heaven.
The mystical secret of Heaven, Earth and Humanity
  manifests before us.
The secret profundity of the spiritual truth
  and the sacred meaning
  of all mystical wonders become clear.
In order to transcend worldly, unrefined customs
  and alleviate all sensory illusions and obstacles,
  the root of life is recaptured,
  and the Integral Way is attained.

When this profound decree is uncovered,
    the clear, bright road can be traveled.
The gold and jade scriptures
    become one's daily influences.
We are deeply grateful for this great fortune.

Verse of Sacred Dedication

We are thankful to be on the path
    of truthful spiritual development.
It alone is the foundation for achieving the Integral Way.
No longer do we wander or stray from the way of Heaven,
    like wandering spirits or homeless ghosts.
The Integral Way is engraved on our bones
    and implanted in our hearts forever.

Those whose self-awareness is high
    know that their spiritual life
    is handed down from Heaven.
They stay connected and in harmony
    with the root of everlasting life,
    which is the true Heaven.
Those who are deluded indulge in shallow desires
    or sink into deceptive, man-made religions.
Only with the help of an achieved one,
    whose teachings are like priceless seeds,
    can one cross over the river of illusion.
Correctly sown and nourished
    with water, air and sunshine,
    they will sprout and bear an abundant harvest.

If spiritually achieved ones did not have the mercy
    to pilot us across the river of life,
    we would never reach the other side.
If we are enabled to cross that river,
    we vow to help others cross it also.
Without the guiding light
    of spiritually achieved ones to help us navigate,
    we would continue to suffer and drown in bitter seas.

By traveling on the integral path
of righteousness and selflessness,
we set an example for others
who wish to travel on it also.
Spiritual descendants of the Universal Achieved Ones
cultivate the light within themselves
so they can manifest their light to help the world.
When one is enlightened,
one can safely guide oneself and others.
Our purpose and duty is to pass on the light
that can help others navigate through life.
As we travel the enlightened path of brightness,
we cast off our old and heavy impurities.
By borrowing from the unreal to cultivate the real
we renew our clarity
so that we can look upon the lives of others as our own,
and regard their mistakes
as if we had made them ourselves.

The world is full of detrimental influences.
Only by following the Universal Way is one able to
embody the Heart of Heaven,
actualize the Will of Heaven,
manifest the Way of Heaven,
plant the seed of eternal wisdom,
continue the teachings of the Universal Way,
cultivate unending virtuous fulfillment,
and strengthen the harmony between Heaven and Earth.

To the generations of achieved ones
who have preserved the teachings of the Universal Way
we vow to become seeds of truth
among all men and women.
We vow, from the bottom of our hearts,
to help those who suffer
learn how to transcend their delusions.
May the Heart of Heaven support us
in opening the correct gate of life
to those who want to save themselves.

Thus the heritage of the Universal Way will not be broken,
the eternal wisdom of the achieved ones will never end,
the teachings of universal oneness will never perish,
and the gate to Heaven will always be open.

The Universal Way is our touchstone.
By following its example,
we learn to respect Heaven and love others.
We correct our own conduct and cultivate ourselves
with diligence and dedication.
Through our own virtuous fulfillment,
we sow the seeds of the Universal Way
of harmony and balance.
This divine tradition is protected by Heaven;
those who forsake their true nature
for meaningless things
cannot receive the sacred methods of the Universal Way.
Thus we do not stray
from the righteousness of our true nature
in pursuit of excessive worldly pleasure or possessions.

Because we are aware that the boundless grace of Heaven
cannot be repaid,
we vow to follow the Universal Way
and continue its sacred methods
of spiritual self-cultivation.
We vow to make ourselves into living shrines
of the integral truth
and become gateways
for those who seek to cross the river.
Those who are virtuous can learn
the sacred methods of spiritually achieving themselves.
Those who are still struggling with worldly self-deceptions
can be directed toward a place
where virtuous beings gather.
By persevering in the cultivation of positive virtues,
one benefits oneself and others.
We offer ourselves as servants of the Universal Way.
We are dedicated to improving ourselves
and cultivating ourselves with sincerity

so that we may unite with
the subtle spiritual truth of Oneness.
and build a ladder to Heaven for all to use.
May we become ships to help others across troubled waters.
May we strive to achieve and gather
the virtuous light of Heaven,
and may it radiate from us
and guide the world to deep fulfillment.

Heaven Loves People

Though the way of Tao seems mysterious and remote,
it responds positively to the virtuous.
This is because people are born and nourished
by the universe.
In return, people should act according to the subtle laws
of the universe.
In order to remain in harmony with the universe
one should not separate oneself from the whole.
Heavenly will is our will.
Heavenly work is our work.
Heavenly nature is not beyond the nature
of its descendants.
We are fortunate enough to know that Heaven is not
separate from our own integral beings.

Tao is transmitted directly from the Subtle Origin,
but the way of cultivating Tao
is handed down by our teachers.
The wisdom of the teacher is Heaven.
We humbly extend the Vow of Heaven
through which our heart may reach
the Heavenly sphere.
Heaven is our spiritual treasure,
always full and abundant.
Our virtue is the most valuable thing among
our wealth and properties.
May the gate of Heaven always be open to us.
May Heavenly grace always be bestowed upon us.

May Heavenly help always be with us.
May Heavenly joy always be firmly with us,
   and Heavenly blessing never depart from us.
May our Heavenly nature be maintained without pretense.
May our hearts rest in the fulfillment of our virtue.
May we be inspired by natural wisdom.
May the Heavenly steed with its invisible wings
   take us into boundless space
   with the expansion of Heaven.
May we always keep the company of Divine Immortals.
May we be showered by inexhaustible
   Heavenly blessing and grace.
May our lives constantly bathe in the divine melody of grace.
May the creativeness of Heaven
   assist our lives unfailingly
   for many generations to come.
All these are Heavenly treasures
   which can be achieved by a sincere heart.
We beseech Heaven to unite with
   the sincere will and good intentions
   of mankind and with all other lives.

Your humble offspring has nothing to offer
   but this uncontaminated heart
   and its Heavenly bestowed virtues.
To understand that the creative nature of Heaven
   begins the world is to fulfill our virtue
   without deviation or divergence.
The Heavenly truth is such that it is up
   to the nature of man to return
   to the Heavenly realm.
Heavenly blessings are connected with the
   creative virtue of positiveness in mankind.
If man has the insight to maintain his original virtue,
   Heavenly blessings manifest naturally.
If man follows the impartial and balanced
   example of the Heavenly will with diligence,
   then there will always be a happy response.
The only obstacle is the relative realm
   of conceptual life.

Our hearts are deeply buried under layers of dusty desire
    which keep the blessings from springing forth
    from our pure heart.
We ask the Heavenly heart to stay with us.
We are deeply aware that to indulge
    in seeking selfish benefit
    diminishes our life being,
    and to indulge in desire is to suffer.
We keep our intentions pure and clear
    so we can express the harmony of Heaven.
We know that blessings come from a Heavenly nature,
    but we have to rely upon ourselves through cultivation.
We recognize our natural virtue as the reassurance
    of our eternal life.
We will accomplish the Heavenly mission
    with a devoted heart.
Therefore, your humble offspring wish to share the blessing
    of Tao with others,
    and allow no wandering desires
    to distract us from this sacred goal.
Humbly, we beseech the highest Divine One
    to inspect our innermost vibration of mind.
All Heavenly beings, kindly watch over us.
Your humble offspring sincerely hope
    that our wishes will be approved.

Our achievement lies in the fulfillment of our Heavenly duty.
May Heaven grant us the blessing
    of working endlessly to improve and renew our lives
    by cleansing the body, mind and spirit
    until they are as pure as spotless snow.
May the perseverance of our Heavenly spirit endure forever.

Pure Heart Offering to the Integral Divine Realm
As T'ai Chi manifests,
  Heaven and Earth spontaneously evolve.
Clear, light chi rises to Heaven,
  and mixed, heavy chi comes down to become Earth.
A person who cultivates oneself in the right way
  can surely become an integrated
  model of Heaven and Earth.
With three thousand good deeds,
  a person would be able to reform their short span of life
  to forty thousand epochs.
The altar of a pure heart's devotion would be disclosed
  with the burning incense in the cauldron,
  and these Golden Chapters would be continued
  in practice for generations to come.

(The offering of incense)

The fragrance of incense fills the Shrine,
  and makes the auspicious chi rise to the sky.
We behold the splendid clouds of East and West,
  and rightfully present our sincerity.
Devotedly, we bow to the Integral Divine Realm.

(Three bows. Set incense in incense holder.)

We dedicate our hearts through the burning of
  this pure, fragrant incense, in accordance with
  the fragrance and light of our virtuous cultivation.

The radiance of our spontaneous response,
  the beams of our unattached clear minds,
  the aura of our self-natured mystical wonders,
  the subtle light of our wisdom
  in this altar of sincerity and piety,
  become completely harmonized with
  all lights of transcendence of the Earthly realms,
  and all lights of the Heavenly realms.

This great harmony of spiritual light
     is reflected as the inner light of our hearts.
We bow and sincerely offer this incense
     with our harmonized inner light,
     to all divine immortals,
     to all ancient achieved ones and to their
     directly and indirectly inspired descendants
     who achieved themselves to enter
     the Heavenly Immortal Realm,
     to those who embrace Heaven
     and serve Tao throughout all time,
     and to those enlightened with brilliant wisdom
     and pure virtue in all eras.
The numerous divine beings who are reached
     with our pure single mind shall respond to us
     anywhere and anytime we have
     their complete awareness.

The Great Path of divine Masters
     and wondrous divine immortals
     guides and supports us.
May our lives be a manifestation
     of the Great Path of One Truth.
May we extend Heaven's kindness in our lives.
May we integrate our lives with the righteousness of Heaven.
May our ancestors, our descendants, our friends
     and everyone be inspired and guided by
     the Great Path of the One Truth.
With great happiness we offer our devotion.

Because we sincerely cultivate ourselves
     and serve people, we can forever bathe
     in the joy of Heavenly blessings.
Let all other beings also receive this blessing.

We offer our life being
     to the integral spiritual realm,
     to the Great One of the Great Divine Path of One Truth,
     to the Great Eternal Body of Truth,
     to the Great One of Universal Natural Wisdom,

to the Great One of all Virtuous Fulfillment,
to the Great One of Eternal Passages of All Formed
    Existence,
to the Great One of the Most Approachable Truth of Life,
to the Great Protector of the Truth of Life,
to the Great Generals, taming the wildness
    of all minds with quietude,
to the Great One of Transmitting the Truth
    of the Universe as One's Life Body,
to the Great One of Integralness of Total Existence,
to the most noble of all common, fundamental beings,
to the truth carriers,
to the messengers of truth,
to the supporters of truth,
to the followers of truth,
to the achieved divine ones
    who successfully opened
    the six spiritual channels of divine abilities
    of sense and mystical responsive power,
to the spiritual messengers of the Nine Palaces,
to the eight manifestations of nature
    which exercise the way of subtle integration,
to the divine lords of the sixty combinations
    of natural energies of Heavenly Stems
    and Earthly Branches
to the Six Ding, universal yin energies,
    as helpful Jade girls,
to the Six Jia, universal yang Energies,
    as Divine Commanders,
to the Six Yen, Yang Water Energies, as wise advisors,
to the Twelve Heavenly guardians,
to the Twelve Heavenly Generals,
to the Thirty-six Heavenly Powers,
to the Seventy-two Earthly Powers,
to the messengers of the Shiens who reach everywhere,
to the Five Divinities of the five directions,
to the angels from the ten directions,
to the executives of the invocations
    and secret spiritual words,

to the Four Meritorious Officials
    of the year, month, day and hour,
to all the true assistant divinities of spiritual practices,
to the Heavenly deities and generals
    who at any time respond to summons and prayers,
to the spiritual troops and generals
    who are ever-responsive,
to the golden-armored deity and golden-winged angels.
As students of Tao we devote ourselves to serving the truth
    and are recognized by these Golden Words.
We all bathe in the love of Heaven.

May divine mercy and subtle virtue be with us.
May our altar manifest Tao and spread the subtle law
    as the virtuous way of eternal life.
With deep sincerity, all responses are reached.

To reach Heaven above and Earth below,
    and to help kind and innocent
    human beings in between,
    we aid the righteous, stop aggression,
    and support the virtuous against evil
    inside and outside our life being.

When people are virtuous, their spiritual practice
    is responded to by the divine realm
    and all their goals can be achieved.

In order to become a vessel of the true path,
    we follow the way of Heavenly blessings,
    which is to give.
Thus beneficial kindness permeates
    all realms of our existence.

As humble students, we unify our hearts and minds
    throughout all lifetimes.
We continue the natural virtue from above
    by diligently achieving subtle divine merit
    and by sincerely offering ourselves to the
    universal life source with utmost respect.

The Golden Palace of Heavenly Beams,
the true center of Heaven's silent expansion,
the very root of Tao,
envelops the manifest and unmanifest,
the beginning and end.
The Jade Emperor is the Heart of the universe
and the true nature of the subtle law.
He is the embodiment of all wonders
and is the true model of all great Masters
and of all Heavenly Immortals.

To Yu Heng Shan Ti, the Supreme One of Great Balance,
we bow.

To the most divine, subtle, and everlasting Heaven,
the origin of all spirits, the source of life,
and the source of the Jade Fountain of healing,
we bow.

To the highly sacred and divine,
the most mystical energy of Heaven,
transformed as the seven original Shiens,
the Big Dipper, the symbol of varying Heavenly order,
we bow.

To the high ruler of mystical Heaven,
the nobly true being of the North Pole,
who is the symbol of the ancient virtuous model
and benevolent Master of the ten thousand spirits,
the kind father of all living beings who eliminates
suffering and forgives all sins,
the great mercy and hope of the world,
the nobly virtuous and benevolent,
the highly divine and deeply merciful,
the sublime harmony of nine Heavens,
the Heavenly divinity who arouses thunder,
the source of all transformation,
we bow.

To the the Subtle Purple Light of the Divine Palace,
the honorable Emperor of
the Sun Palace and Moon Mansion,
the five stars of the sun rays,
the Northern and Southern stars,
the Big Dipper and Tien Li (Heavenly Law),
the uncountable stars in Heaven,
the administrator of yin and yang,
the maintainer of law in the universe,
the king of all stars in the Jade Heaven,
the ruler of the evolution of lives,
the supreme Queen of Creation,
the Emperor above the North Pole,
we bow.

To the primal undivided Oneness of all Heavens,
the disseminating King of Law
who transmits teachings and possesses
the foremost awareness of the human realm
to aid and pilot the suffering of the multitudes,
who assists in cultivating the truth and
awareness of Tao to benefit all under Heaven,
and dispenses with disasters and obstacles,
who possesses eighty-two ways of transformation,
we bow.

To the brilliant Shiens of all teachings,
the Great Masters of the truthful tradition,
we bow.

To the benevolent and merciful ones who save us
from suffering and cast away hardship,
the overall supervisors of the three realms
of Heaven, Earth, and Man,
the diligent messengers who roam in the high Heavens,
we bow.

To the powerful stars,
>   starting with the Big Dipper, and on its right and left,
>   the guards of Heavenly law and supporters of truth,
>   the Great Generals, helpers of the world and people
>   we bow.

To the Heavenly Guard and the aid of Heavenly movement,
>   the true power and divine responsive energy
>   which bless the virtuous and spread happiness,
>   the true spirits of kindness and righteousness,
>   and supporters of the virtuous individual's fate,
>   we bow.

To the blessing spirit and unruling ruler of the world,
>   the virtuous, formless minister of Yu Shu,
>   minister of evil-quelling, who is the
>   transformer of the Golden Palace,
>   we bow.

To the mysterious Heaven of universal sovereignty,
>   the divine court of the Purple Light Empire,
>   the guards of law within the three realms of existence,
>   the sole ruler of ten thousand spirits,
>   we bow.

To the Heavenly virtue expressed as Heavenly deities,
>   the subtle rays of purple light that
>   confer all blessings and respond to our hearts,
>   we bow.

To the sublime Earthly deities who pardon people's
>   transgressions and forgive their mistakes,
>   the divinity that responds to our mind
>   of broadness and impartiality,
>   we bow.

To the sublime virtuous energy of delivery,
>   the official of relieving distress, the divinity of seeing
>   the unseeable who responds to our conduct,
>   we bow.

To the Master governors of the three Primal Realms,
   the thirty-six thousand most responsive deities,
   who provide for everything all the time,
   who listen to prayers and respond to sincerity,
   we bow.

To the numberless and boundless golden armor spirits,
   Heavenly kings, Heavenly generals,
   Star generals, Star lords, and Star deities,
   we bow.

To the numberless and boundless
   Heavenly lords, Divine lords,
   spiritual messengers, Heavenly ambassadors,
   Star Shiens and Star Spirits,
   we bow.

To the female Shiens and truly integral beings,
   inquisitive spirits and spiritual officials,
   barefoot immortals,
   and all other graceful beings,
   we bow.

To all the nameable and unnameable Shiens,
   the happy immortals,
   together we are harmonized
   with true sincerity as a universal offering.

With sincere virtue we devotedly offer our pure heart
   in complement to the divine influences
   which are ever manifesting and responsive.
Our own lives are also the complement of the
   divine blessing of longevity.
 We further ask for mercy for the turmoil of the world,
   and pity upon the misfortunes
   caused by human mischief.
Good and evil are distinguished
   in the books of the three Primal Realms.
Honor the pure of heart and protect the disciplined.
Reply to sincere prayers with joy.

Eliminate disasters and dispel sins.
Send blessings from Heaven and lengthen our lives.
This is the work of the most truly
*   divine and wondrous being.*
The merits of virtue are bestowed upon all,
*   especially the benevolent and aspiring,*
*   the nobly virtuous and kind.*

Please allow us, the students of truth,
*   to aid the true law and offer the*
*   Divine Way as a guide for the ignorant.*
With this virtue, we can face all the divine beings and
*   Grand Masters at the meetings of all Heavenly Shiens*
*   in the high spiritual mountains when*
*   gathering for spiritual achievement.*
We extend ourselves to be a spiritual shelter and
*   aid to all so that our cultivation and service are*
*   evidence of the Heavenly Law that realizes*
*   benefit to others from a pure heart.*
Thus we can obtain the correct fruits of our cultivation.

May our hearts be pure, harmonious and peaceful.

May our Great Truth flourish and our worldly work
*   be prosperous and not offended by evil.*
May all auspicious blessings be conferred.
May the benefits of yin and yang abundantly aid our being
*   and may we always be sheltered by Heaven.*

Divine virtue and Heavenly love permeate our lives.
As the fragrance and clouds from the invisible
*   incense of my heart spread luxuriously,*
*   so do everlasting blessings from Heaven.*
With devotion we meet the most supreme
*   of all Heavenly Shiens.*
From five directions descends true chi,
*   bringing with it a hundred blessings.*
All disasters are eliminated and
*   ten thousand miseries vanish.*

The spirits of the Three Origins protect us,
    and the eyes of ten thousand Shiens watch over us.
Our lives are peaceful and trouble free
    because we unite our hearts and minds
    with the eternal Tao.
The universal will and our will become one.

Because our younger brothers, sisters,
    sons and daughters follow the Tao
    and use this tradition as their vantage point,
    divine spiritual beings often visit our Shrine.
With one hundred salutations,
    we are bathed in divine energy forever.
We pray that our longevity will be boundless
    and our spiritual effectiveness will continue eternally.

Our life being resides with the everlasting
    life beings of all divinities.
All divinities live within our spiritual being.
This is our spiritual vision, purified and unified.
This is our spiritual reality.
This is our direction.

Chapter 9

Cultivation Is a Lifetime Process

Be Clear about Your Spiritual Direction

Most religions impose strict disciplines on their followers in order to placate their emotional needs. Since most of these organizations are more social than spiritual, transcending the ego or relative world is difficult. Also, the intellect and emotions are so strongly emphasized that reaching beyond the temporal in order to experience the infinite, unchanging Oneness becomes almost hopeless. These religions merely substitute one illusion for another.

Since before recorded history, the true spiritual method of simplicity, calmness and ease has been handed down to us by our teachers. These teachings are not overly concerned with the relative world and may not appear as colorful as others; nevertheless they do lead more directly to the highest levels of spirit.

Even the attainment of many wonderful spiritual experiences should be seen only as the beginning, because those levels of achievement are limited. Each experience can only be considered as another phenomenon of the great wholeness that is Tao. With this understanding, one will not be misguided to be egotistic by partial spiritual experiences or by any religion that only encourages partial development.

Twelve Fundamental Principles of Self-Development

1. *Tao is the Subtle Origin and Primal Energy of the universe.* We recognize the Subtle Origin of the universe as the Mysterious Mother of existence and non-existence. The universe is naturally so; it was neither created nor designed. Even though there is no personified creator, Tao - the primal energy which exercises and develops itself - brings forth all manifestations of the universe. The original energy becomes the subtle law of its manifestation. Everything manifested and unmanifested is a spontaneous expression of the nature of the Subtle Origin; no intentional design is needed.

The universe is an energy network of its own connectedness. All individual beings and things are under the influence of the energy net in the vast arena of the universe. The energy net is the natural administrative system. The freedom of all things and beings is prescribed exactly. If we indulge in our strong passions, emotions, desires and ambitions, the influence of the energy net will be very strong. If our energy is light, the influence of the energy net will also be light. If we lead normal lives, in harmony with the universe, we will see no sign of the existence of an energy net at all. In this universe, each life is responsible for itself.

Nobody can assign an external God to be his savior. However, spiritual aid will sometimes come in the form of kind and highly evolved persons or natural beings who stretch out helping hands. A person may also have good fortune when his energy moves into a favorable cycle. Great awareness is needed to discern whether a person is really being helped in spiritual growth or whether he is just responding to the illusion of religious enthusiasm caused by emotional indulgence.

2. *The existence of Tao is absolute.* Whether one is aware of Tao or not, all beings receive their life energy from Tao. Some follow the subtle law consciously, while others follow it unconsciously. Yet with or without awareness, Tao is the essence of all life. To be ignorant of Tao, the subtle truth, is to live in blindness. To know Tao is to see clearly. Therefore, we follow only the absolute, nameless, original Oneness of the universe, which is the essence of our life. If we violate Tao, we annihilate our own life. We cannot exist without Tao. We reject all man-made names and religious concepts which were created for a second-rate mind. They confuse and obstruct our direct experience of truth. The Integral Way is gentle. Brute force is the low-level of some religions, but it is never the spiritual truth of a high being.

3. *Our inner intention is to clarify and purify our own spirit. Our outer intention is to extend care and kindness to all beings and things.* We refine our emotions and desires to be

as light as possible in order to maintain ourselves as a high level being. We do not indulge in passionate love or hate. Temper and passion are by no means our ruler. In this way we avoid any downfall. We also avoid religious emotionalism. As a spiritual child, religious emotionalism may function to initiate one's journey back to the Source. However, as a spiritual adult, religious emotionalism will prevent direct union with Tao. To follow Tao, the subtle law, is to follow the integration of the universe with harmonious life-giving energy. To follow religious emotion is to form prejudice and nurture hostility, and as a consequence, invite death.

4. *We practice conservation in our lives, particularly with regard to our energy.* We do not scatter our energy or distract our minds with frivolous, unnecessary activities. We avoid wasting energy through arguments, restless nonsense (busy work), fidgety behavior, and meddling in the affairs of others. In this way we preserve the integrity of our spirit and enjoy harmony with the universe. We keep a hermit's spirit in a busy worldly life.

5. *We bravely and earnestly face the truth of life.* We do not undertake spiritual cultivation as an escape from the reality of life, as may be the case in some religions. A simple, plain and natural life is essential to spiritual completeness. *Wu Wei*, or the way of non-contention, is our highest discipline.

6. *We follow the constant virtue and normalcy of the universe as the model of our life.* The guideline of a spiritual life is to keep a clear mind and have few desires.

7. *We practice neither asceticism nor wantonness.* We enjoy the beauty, richness and nobility of life, and we practice the principles of right purpose, right method and right timing according to the universal subtle law of energy response. This sacred spiritual tradition can be maintained only by those who lead disciplined, simple and righteous lives. Initially, discipline is rendered by the teacher to

awaken the disciple. An aspect of self-discipline is abstinence from drugs, coffee and excessive consumption of alcohol and other similar substances which are obstacles to spiritual refinement. Later, the developed individual is guided directly by Tao.

8. *Sincerity, purity of heart and good deeds can lift an ordinary life to the divine realm.* However, we do not disrupt the simplicity of life to create artificial opportunities to do good. This kind of effort is unnecessary, for a simple life is divine in itself. To learn Tao, fundamentally, is to live a simple, natural, and essential life. It means we deny trivialities and avoid unnecessary activities. In this way, we integrate our spirit.

9. *The Teachers of this ancient tradition of Tao and of Ch'an (also spelled Zahn or Zen) are our spiritual pioneers and examples.*

10. *The clarity, purity and harmony of your own energy is the reality of union with Tao.* Heavy energy (including emotional force and psychological cloudiness) is an obstruction to true spiritual growth. The teaching of spiritual cultivation is broader than limited religious teachings. Most religions depend on the psychological weakness of human beings. Some use mass hypnosis in the attempt to help control people's cloudy minds. They mistake emotionalism for spirit. Thus, most religions foster self-assertiveness, prejudice, development of ego, and hostility, which are spiritual pitfalls. Sons and daughters of Tao must be above this and all things. Spiritual cultivation integrates one's being with the wholeness of the universe.

11. *Sanity is the essential foundation for learning Tao.* It is also the basis for the development and subjective evolution of one's own being. Without a sound body and mind there is no hope of attaining Tao, the subtle origin. The temporal phenomenon of madness is not encouraged in the path of spiritual cultivation. Criminal stories, ghost stories, or even most religious stories are not food for a good mind.

12. *We adopt Master Ni's works as the modern elucidation of the teaching of the ancient achieved ones.* Those who accept the above spiritual principles are recognized by this tradition as its spiritual heirs.

The Necessary Qualities
of a True Student of Spiritual Development

Are your spiritual roots firmly and deeply planted
*   in the Tao?*
Are you truly virtuous and sincere?
Are you willing to transform yourself
*   and eliminate all negative attitudes and habits?*
Are you willing to build
*   a stable and broad personality?*
Are you willing to plunge yourself
*   into the sacred ocean of natural spiritual culture*
*   and aspire to become an achieved one?*
If a student is without these essential qualities,
*   even if the highest methods of Tao*
*   are passed along, he or she will not understand them*
*   or derive any benefit from them.*
On the contrary, spiritual growth may be impeded.

The Correct Attitude
of a True Student of Spiritual Development

A good student humbly and gratefully
*   accepts the teacher*
*   in order to go straightly forward*
*   on the path of Tao.*
With love, gratitude, and sincerity
*   the student respectfully accepts*
*   instruction from the teacher.*
The student faithfully follows,
*   serves and obeys the teacher,*
*   who is the embodiment of Tao.*
The student should be willing to dedicate his mind,
*   his spirit, and even his whole being*
*   to the teacher and his teaching.*

Only a spiritually mature student
can recognize the teacher as he truly is.
A student who is foolish enough
to rely only on cleverness
will endlessly go around and around
in the false illusions of ego.
A student who remains single-purposed
and unceasing in his self-cultivation
will surely attain the goal
of true spiritual achievement.

Qualities of a True Teacher

A teacher is a Heavenly Shien
who has come to live in the world.
He is the Tao become a human being.
He is a spiritual light to all those in darkness,
and the embodiment of divine energy.
To be with him is to experience living Truth.
He is the revelation of the mystery
of Heaven, Earth and Man.
He has fully developed and integrated
all aspects of his being.
His life is an expression of wisdom and pure law.
He has unconditional love for all lives.
His smile radiates light, wisdom and bliss.
His mind is as deep and all-encompassing
as the Tao.
He has transcended the mystery of life and death,
and has broken the dream-like quality
of his own mental faculty.
His personal nature is one with the Tao.
His speech and behavior are the fruit
of his own spiritual attainment,
responding to the personalities
and environments he encounters.
He teaches selflessly,
not out of a desire
for self-aggrandizement.

He is the true father, true mother,
*   true brother and true friend*
*   of his students.*
His grace always shines on them,
*   illuminating the dark corners*
*   of their minds.*
He shares his divine energy with them,
*   and is always aware of their problems.*
He dissolves their pain in his ocean
*   of compassion.*
Before his eyes he sees
*   only the true nature of his students.*
And when they are ready
*   to give up their false pretenses,*
*   their sadness, imperfections and*
*   false personalities quickly fade away.*
He knows the traps and obstacles of life,
*   and can guide a student*
*   out of troubled waters*
*   if the student is wise enough*
*   to take his precious guidance.*
His lion's roar scoldings
*   awaken students who are lost.*
A teacher can awaken the students'
*   divine energy and lead him or her*
*   to enlightenment.*
He can direct their stream of life
*   into the infinite ocean of Tao.*

The purpose of the teaching of Tao is not to establish a
rigid relationship between teacher and student, leader and
follower, or to make people belong to one thing or another.
Neither is it intended to create obligations or commitments
outside of teachings. A real spiritual relationship is not
limited by form or protocol; formlessness is an important
characteristic of true spiritual teachings. Only through self-
cultivation did the great ones achieve. Being natural and
original and not attaching to form is where spiritual truth
can be found.

When You Have the Opportunity
to be Close to a Truly Achieved Teacher

In order not to abuse the opportunity which enables you to learn the spiritual truth from a true teacher of natural spiritual truth, some suggestions are given below for those of you who wish to obtain the benefit from making him or her your spiritual symbol.

When you have a question concerning the techniques of your self-cultivation: Extend the most important question in your mind directly. He or she will then respond to you accordingly and effectively.

When you have an important spiritual problem concerning your life or your understanding, or when you have an urgent question that needs an immediate response: All books of the same teacher, if he or she is truly achieved, will answer you where and when it is right. You will receive the answers by reading.

Do not bother the teacher of spiritual achievement with trivial matters: The teacher should not have to concern himself with such things. He maintains a spirit of unstained innocence and simplicity and one should respectfully avoid troubling him with the complicated matters of worldly life. To the beginner who is still entangled in the snares of the world and his own emotions, all things however small seem large. If you bother the teacher with such matters, you will receive no answer. The answers to these kinds of problems should come through one's own cultivation and work on oneself. Never complain if the teacher does not take your problems away, for they are your own manifestation.

Do not use worldly techniques to approach a teacher: You may flatter him and he would accept your flattery. You may bribe him and he would probably take the gift innocently. You may offer your favors to him and he may accept them. All of these are worldly approaches. In this way you can touch the teacher's worldly aspects, but you will not get to the precious truth. The only way one can gain true benefit from him is by making oneself more receptive through faithful, loyal, stable and consistent cultivation. Through self-achievement, your spiritual eyes and ears will open. With sharpened sensitivity you will become closer to him. However, the teacher's spiritual attainment is different from yours, so the Heavenly level where he truly resides is also different. You can try to understand some aspects of the teacher, but only through stable, consistent cultivation will the higher levels gradually become known.

Do not use worldly criteria in an attempt to understand or explain the teacher: A teacher looks quite ordinary and not very different from yourself. How much you will know of him depends upon your own mental and spiritual abilities. These abilities grow according to your own self-discipline and cultivation. The more they grow, the more responsive he can be to your life and cultivation. You can do this with only two virtues: love and respect. Love without respect may impede your own spiritual evolution. Respect without love will never allow you to become close enough to him to receive the Light of Wisdom for your sanctification.

Do not try to use the teacher for selfish or egotistical purposes: Students should never try to use the teacher's spiritual achievement or reputation for their own self-aggrandizement or ask the teacher to do something for them. In other words, do not make the teacher your servant. Most advanced students know that the teacher's presence alone is enough to calm their mind and dissolve their illusions, for the teacher, who is a living symbol of simplicity and empathy for all, has a thorough understanding of them. The main concern of a good student is only how best to serve and follow the teacher rather than what he or she can get from him. Their relationship is simply the spirit of selfless service. With this spirit one can swim in the spiritual ocean of grace of all past teachers.

Do not hold any preconceived notions about the teacher: To have any notions that the teacher should be this way or that is to invite confusion and disappointment. The teacher is a natural and spontaneous being. This means that you can never be sure how he will react in any given circumstance. Being a clear reflection of all that goes on around him, he is quite capable of reflecting your highest or your lowest states. To see him is often to see the reflection of your own worst traits. In these circumstances, the teacher is allowing you to see and deal with your weaknesses and character flaws through him, so do not doubt his instruction or subtle suggestion. Keep an open, trustful mind at all times, and your cultivation will proceed smoothly.

Serve the teacher selflessly: The teacher is a manifestation of your own spirit. He exists within you and you exist within him. He encourages your spirit to be selfish in the correct way, i.e., through selflessness. To selflessly serve the teacher is ultimately to serve yourself. This is the key to putting yourself into the mainstream of the Eternal Tao. Through this process you will experience that the relationship with the teacher is not only person to person, but a unification of yourself with the past, present and future of the universe. In other words, to be in harmony with the teacher is to be in harmony with life itself. Being good to the teacher is the first and last step in your life of spiritual cultivation and discipline. By holding onto this principle firmly, you will have a smooth and successful life as a student of high spiritual truth and you will realize the three spiritual realms: the Heaven of Great Purity, the Heaven of Crystal Purity, and the Heaven of Utmost Purity, manifesting in your life. You will fulfill your sacred destiny and rank as a *Shien* in the Heavenly Family.

The subtle influence of the teacher's power will come only when a student has a sincere, honest and receptive spirit. Do not be too forceful, whether negatively or positively, because such strong energy interferes with his subtle influence. Do not urge him to do anything for you, but instead let him respond when the time is right.

His power cannot be used for individual purposes. His power is the manifestation of the divine energy of the universe which is pure, stainless and without inclinations or preferences. Only in this way can he efficiently and effectively produce the right response in the right person. An impure desire to use this highest power to benefit only oneself can never be fulfilled. To summon a teacher of Heaven or Earth, you must remember this basic principle or else your prayers will be in vain and you will unnecessarily limit yourself. To be selfish is to be against the true nature of Tao.

The Tao Guan (Spiritual Retreat)

A *Tao Guan* is a place, though it literally means to observe your life objectively. It might seem to resemble a church or monastery but in fact is not anything like either one. It is rather a workshop, a living fountain and a small universe. It is not limited to only one aspect of life. Positive endeavors can originate in and flourish from the spiritual nurturing found in a *Tao Guan*. It usually consists of a few buildings, a garden, classrooms, a healing center and herb room, and is always centered around a shrine. The shrine invites harmonious interchange with natural spirits and deities. It also gives recognition to such human qualities as morality, decency, sanity, independence, mellowness, love of nature, universal love and other positive virtues.

How to Use the Shrine
to Be More Beneficial to Your Spiritual Practice

Build the shrine with the same respect you would show your own sublime beingness. It should be treated as a sacred place; an oasis of good energy. People who are highly sensitive are at once aware of the power and sacredness of the subtle energy of a shrine when they enter it.

When entering, bow to the center of the shrine. This salutation is an offering of respect and humility to the spiritual world and to the achieved immortal beings of our spiritual lineage. A careless attitude can literally close the channels of receptivity and greatly lessen the experience of internal guidance.

If it is necessary to speak in the shrine, speak softly with sensitivity so as not to disturb others. The shrine is not a place to gossip or carry on conversations.

Do not lie down in the shrine. Do not extend your feet toward the center of the shrine or the teacher, and do not turn your back to the shrine.

Everything in the shrine has its proper place. Do not move the sacred instruments without permission. They are never to be used as playthings.

Do not sit in the teacher's chair.

Do not engage in any discussion of a trivial nature. The shrine is a place of sharing in spirit and subtle energy.

Do not lead guests who do not have respect into the shrine. The results of such disrespectful intrusions are serious.

Never bring pets into the shrine.

The responsibility to protect the sacredness of the shrine lies in your sincerity of heart.

Wherever a shrine is, the immortals of our long tradition come to help and guide the spiritual cultivation of their spiritual descendants.

All three great realms reside within the shrine: the Great Origin of Purity, the great Origin of Clarity, and the Great Origin of Harmony.

How to Arrange Your Personal Shrine

A personal shrine serves to develop your connection with the high spiritual realms. To set up your shrine the following guidelines are recommended.

Choose a nice, clean place in your home that will remain undisturbed. Locate the shrine in the center of this area and in an elevated position. The symbols used in the Shrine represent the divinities of the three spiritual realms. The covers of Master Ni's first three books in English were chosen to serve this purpose and can be placed on stands to occupy a central place on the table or shelf. Offerings of fruits or flowers are placed in front of the divinities.

Keep the shrine simple and uncluttered. Only the highest, most sublime images of the immortal tradition of Tao should be used. To complete your shrine, a portrait of Master Lu, Tung Ping or another highly achieved immortal can be placed above the altar[1], or you may use any other symbol that spiritually uplifts you.

Expressions of the Integral Way of Life
1. We are not a vulgar religion that tempts people with external spiritual promises.

2. We are a transreligious integral path of universal truth.

3. We follow this path with the purpose of achieving universal subtle integration, the great oneness expressed as Tao.

4. Our path is not a new invention, and neither is it a new mixture of all the old. It is the high guidance of the Universal Divine Realm through the self-awareness of achieved people of all generations.

5. We transcend all discriminating names and concepts and reach directly for the unnameable reality of universal subtle truth.

6. We exalt no particular image or doctrine, but follow the eternal truth of universal Oneness.

7. We do not focus on worldly confusion, but direct our attention to spiritual integration, the dissolving of our self.

8. Our way does not involve itself in discrimination and partialities which fragment human nature and disharmonize our involvement in life. Nor do we create any alienation by insisting on integral mindedness. We see the world not through fragmented vision, but through the integral view.

9. We ask no commitment from anyone who joins us. We offer ourselves to universal love. For this reason, we offer ourselves to all humanity.

10. These statements are not external commandments imposed upon us, but expressions of our own deep awareness and our willingness to follow that awareness.

The Spiritual Origin and Teaching of the Integral Way

Integral beings are spiritual immortals. These subtle beings exist in realms that transcend time and space. They were the first beings to come from the pure, creative energy of the Subtle Origin of the universe which existed long before the creation of Heaven and Earth.

The Integral Beings have continuously exerted a subtle influence, not only on mankind and earthly events, but also on the events of the entire universe. Since the beginning of time, all things are constantly changing under the universal law of transformation. Only the immeasurable Integral Beings are beyond degeneration because of their continuous, instantaneous renewal through self-mastery.

In the beginning, the Earth was uninhabited. The original beings from the Subtle Origin of the universe combined themselves with the *yin*, or physical energy, of the Earth and thus gave birth to mankind. Naturally, they became the earliest, true ancestors of the human race. The first inhabitants of Earth were faithful to their divine nature, so it was not necessary for them to cultivate or discipline themselves. They spontaneously enjoyed full, effective lives without needing to use intellectual functions. Because their energy was pure and complete they did not require self-refinement. They lived long and abundant lives. However, after many generations passed, mankind began to degenerate and their subtle, divine energy gradually dissipated. It became necessary for human beings to develop their intellect to compensate for the loss of ability to respond spontaneously to the environment.

Humankind has within itself the divine essence from the Subtle Origin, but during the course of history its divinity has been covered over by many layers of mental creations, acquisitions and confusion. Originally, the mind was the intermediary of the spirit and the physical body, but because its role became overplayed, it overpowered the main pillars of human existence, i.e., spirit and the physical body. As a result, humanity has become progressively out of balance and harmony. It became necessary for mankind to invent moral ethics and religion to rectify prevalent negative thinking and behavior. Many religious and social doctrines were created in an attempt to reestablish order and harmony in people's lives. The more the intellect is developed, the less spiritually effective mankind becomes, until people can no longer help themselves spiritually. The byproduct of the overly developed mind are endless calamities.

Through transgression of the laws of nature, unfortunate events happen to people like waves on a stormy sea which make them more and more entangled in negativity. During the early stages of development, when humanity was still uncorrupted, the High Beings frequently descended to Earth and befriended its inhabitants. After the human mind became spoiled, the High Beings made only brief visits to Earth in an attempt to rescue mankind and subtly change the destiny of the world. They come to the world and take human form in order to teach the most virtuous people the way back to their divine origin and to try to protect all people from the negativity which has arisen as a result of the loss of their subtle divine energy.

The Integral Beings who were our first ancestors are the divine origin of humanity. Even though their example and teachings have been scattered down through the ages, their tradition has not been entirely lost. We can still obtain the most precious enlightenment enabling us to free ourselves from the bondage and attraction to our illusions, and at the same time restore ourselves to the simplicity and integrity of our natural being. The Integral Beings' teachings are left in the world as a ferry to help people cross their own troubled waters. The choice of disciples is very strict. Only those with the highest degree of sincerity and willingness to accept responsibility for their own spiritual evolution can be received by this sacred tradition. Only through purification and self-refinement can one hope to attain self-transcendence and completely unite with Tao.

Every level of existence expresses its own particular nature as a result of the specific energy formation it contains. For example, some beings are suited to live in air, some in water, and so forth. However, all beings are produced from the same creative, generating energy of the universe which is generally referred to as Tao. All manifestations are offspring of this primal energy, the subtle source of the universe. Each classification of energy formation exists as a universe unto itself, with its own measurement and awareness or unawareness of time and space.

The principal classifications of energy formation are the spiritual realm, the mental realm, humanity and Earth, all of which comprise the vast universe. The human body, as a microcosm of the universe, contains and thereby is connected with all three principal classifications of energy formation. The head embodies Heaven, or spirit; the middle part or the chest embodies Man, or mind; and the lower part of the trunk (the lower abdomen) embodies Earth, or physical energy. Another way of describing this would be to say that spirit is the core, mind is the undergarment, and the physical body is the overcoat.

Tao reveres the Divine Primacy, the creative energy of the universe. This energy is the highest of all Heavens and is the originator of the harmonious order of the universe. It is the subtle law of the universe and the divine nature of all creation. It is Tao. There are many forms of energy in the universe. The original, creative energy has twisted and distorted itself into many different reflections. These reflections are not the Tao. All phenomena are the offspring of this subtle, generating energy which in ancient times was revered and titled *Ti*, the stem or stalk of the total universal existence, or later the Jade Emperor, the undecayed one. It is only the Tao which this divine tradition reveres.

From the original divine substance came all the variations of the universe. The Integral Beings were the first manifestations of this original, creative energy. They are the most essential and respected beings in the universe. The number of beings is unknowable. According to the law of energy response, if there is a difficulty, High Beings pave the way to the solution. However, the frequency of one's energy must be the same frequency as that of the Integral Beings in order to obtain a response from them. This stream of eternal spirit responds to the divine way of self-cultivation whereby one can refine one's energy to become the same quality as that of the Heavenly Immortals.

It is necessary to have the guidance of a Master or teacher's energy which is truly responsive to the Integral Realm so that the sacred method of spiritual immortality may be passed to us, enabling us to refine ourselves, achieve the fullness of our true divine nature and connect ourselves with the Integral Realm. Thus we can enjoy an eternal life of happiness. The man or woman who is chosen to be a disciple of this divine tradition must be earnest and sensitive. The sacred method is esoteric and cannot be passed to people with unstable virtue. All offerings must be made out of sincerity and service to the teacher and must be done with utmost respectfulness to the Heavenly *Shiens*. The teacher lives in this world as a ferry to mankind and as a spiritual ocean of the universe.

In this book I have outlined the goals for a good modern student of spiritual cultivation. There are five things that one who follows the Natural Path needs to learn. The first is the natural knowledge of life, which includes diet and daily regimen. I have given the basic information on both of these subjects in my second book, *Tao, the Subtle Universal Law*, in the diet class in Book I of *8,000 Years of Wisdom* and in references in several other books.

The second thing is the principle of integration. Rather than valuing only one part of life, people of Integral Truth value life in its totality. Some religious paths only value what they call spiritual and discard the physical or material sphere. Eventually they end up being more materialistic than anyone else. Generally speaking, everyone is rooted in the material sphere and no one can neglect it. For this reason, the teaching of Tao always takes the integral path. On the physical level you might learn *Dao-In* (energy channeling), *Chi Kung (Chi Gong)*, or some other energy guidance such as the Eight Treasures or *T'ai Chi*.[2] Whatever your practice, just be sure that it does not move in the direction of a martial art. Work only for your spiritual integration and follow the principles I have recommended in my books, and you will be safe.

The third thing is to work for natural wisdom. Many people live in darkness and cannot see things clearly because of formalized concepts and emotions which are meaningless for the most part and only obstruct the truth. My other books will help ignite your inner light and guide you in breaking through psychological confusion and the obscurity of your spiritual blind spots. For those who already live in the light, there is no such thing as wisdom or enlightenment. When you bring the high truth down to the expressible level, they appear to have a cause and thus become relative. In the highest levels, there is no such thing as darkness or enlightenment.

The fourth thing is pure spiritual practice as recommended in this book and in my other books. Here I give the basic formula, but not the exact procedures, such as what needs to be done first, what needs to be done second, how long it must be practiced, and in what kind of environment, etc. The treasure map is already in your hands. While you have an opportunity to learn the procedures of spiritual cultivation, your work on this book can lead you to strengthen your spiritual being, and help to establish self-protection from the attack of evil spirits. You still have the possibility of reaching your spiritual goals. Your achievement depends on how serious and concentrated you are in working on your own spiritual development. When the time comes, with the knowledge of the correct procedures, in only forty-nine days you can become aware of your spiritual organs, make them serviceable, and even verify the existence of the spiritual realm. However, I see no value in the demand for quick results or quick knowledge just for the sake of knowing. You still need to continue to practice even after reaching the goal.

[2]See Master Ni's videotapes and books on these movements.

The fifth thing pertains to sexual practices. When you have sexual relations, how should you do it? This knowledge can benefit your whole life, not just your sex life. For the general public I already made my recommendations in *8,000 Years of Wisdom, Book II*. Another publication, *Harmony: the Art of Life*, also serves this purpose.

All the material I have put here is to assist you in building a foundation. It will especially strengthen your virtuous fulfillment and aid in concentration. The establishment of one's true spiritual body and contact with the spiritual world can result within forty to fifty years. After these achievements, the discipline is different and more strict. It must be this way because an untrained mind could suffer from too much exposure to the spiritual world and the many unknowable challenges that await the aspirant. If all these conditions are met, then true spiritual achievement is at hand.

These five lines of discipline and achievement, if worked through, can prepare you for not only a new life, but an immortal spiritual life.

The Spiritual Importance of Chi

Because all of the practices in this book involve *chi*, I want you to thoroughly understand what it is that you are cultivating. Many modern people have misconceptions about the cultivation of *chi*. People tend to overtrust doing jogging, swimming, and other sports as exercise for physical health. They tend to make the body react mechanically. Specifically, overdoing gym exercises can dull one's spiritual sensitivity. You might think you feel something special, but if you give up physical exercises and do exercises that cultivate *chi*, you can experience a kind of transcendent experience. Because they are used to exercises which are mainly physical, people feel that practices like *T'ai Chi* and sitting cultivation cannot possibly help the body much. They even refer to some silent cultivations as wishy-washy, which is an inaccurate observation based only on external appearances. Actually, the nurturing of *chi* that goes on in all silent cultivations is much more beneficial to life than only doing physical exercise. These cultivations work not only on the physical level, but the mental and spiritual levels as well.

As I mentioned, our main work is to grow and nurture *chi*. *Chi* is a person's integral life energy. In a human life, the most essential thing is spirit, but between the spirit and the body is the *chi* of vital energy. The popularly recognized acupuncture channels are channels for *chi*. *Chi* is the main element of our health, thus its refinement is of prime importance in spiritual cultivation.

Chi is also an unformed substance of the body or a spirit. Vegetables have fiber bodies, animals have flesh bodies, and spirits have *chi* bodies. Spirits communicate to humans through the *chi* of the person, not through the sense organs. Higher *chi* is also included in the spirit of one's own being after achievement. In our cultivations, we use the strength and power of the gross or coarse foundation of the physical body to produce *chi*. Then after refinement, it becomes *Shien*, or a free and happy spirit. This is not a fantasy, it is a spiritual fact. All achieved ones not only know it, but actually are it.

To learn *chi*, all the positions and postures I recommended in this book can help you. Among other practices such as meditation, *Dao-In*, Eight Treasures and *T'ai Chi* movement, the main effect, whether moving or still, is not your muscles but the effect of *chi* on the entire body. *Chi* makes the bones and tendons strong, and the muscles flexible. *Chi* is produced from the combination of nerve connections and physical strength, and from the secretions of the glands. When a gland is deficient, people typically take artificial hormones, but in spiritual practices, the glands are stimulated to regenerate themselves and thereby balance the secretions to harmonize with each other. I put it this way to help beginners understand, but *chi* is actually much higher and more subtle than this.

Chi is not limited to bodily movement; it can project to remote distances. If an achieved one thinks warm, then he or she feels warm. This is one phenomenon of *chi*. *Chi* is not only warm, it is indescribable because it is already at the subtle level. It is inaudible, invisible, intangible. *Chi* is the mother of everything. All lives come from the vital *chi* of the universe. The universe itself is a form of life. It is itself the grandest expression of vital *chi*. A good student of the *Tao Teh Ching* can recognize that cultivating Tao is cultivating *chi*. Tao does not need cultivating; it is the *chi* in our body that makes our own spiritual universe. It is not different from the whole universe.

Universal vitality is the correct way of expressing primal *chi*, but where does that vitality come from? At the subtle level, vitality is *chi*. At the level of life, physical force is usually more gross and recognizable. With *chi* we have life. When someone dies, it is because the *chi* leaves the body. All food is different kinds of *chi* at the subtle level. No life can avoid taking in *chi* to sustain itself.

The human body can also produce *chi*. The subtle *chi* can be directly supportive of life. You understand that the center and essence of life is *chi*. Once you have *chi*, you have life. Once you lose it, you lose your life. Therefore, spiritual cultivation nurtures *chi*. The ancient achieved ones did not depend on the science of nutrition to survive. There were no vitamins during their long and healthy lives. Some schools of ancient spiritual practice even reject the intake of food completely. They utilize air and natural energy to sustain their life. I do not emphasize such difficult practices here, but I offer this knowledge as an example of how to surpass physical limitations. However, there is still the need of the material sphere. Yet you can see that the achieved ones had a different path of survival.

Most men and women depend on too many external kinds of exercise and nutrition. Some achieved ones use few material things to support themselves. They prefer to nurture their *chi*, and it turns back to sustain their health. People who nurture their *chi* have no need to engage in any strong exercise or strenuous movement. This foundation of *chi* is the entire system of silent, gentle cultivation.

My recommendations to beginners come from my real experience. It is easy to know *chi* when you learn *T'ai Chi*, but do not carry it to the extreme of physical combat. That is the wrong way to use *chi*.

From *chi*, the universe comes alive. From a little *chi* we obtain our life. The *chi* is gathered and starts shaping in the womb, and after departure from the mother, it becomes stronger and stronger until one day, if one cannot keep the *chi*, the *chi* does not keep you, either. You lose your life. You can attain wealth, but money cannot buy *chi*. This is why for a practitioner of spiritual cultivation, *chi* is gathered and nurtured in every moment of life.

Modern people pay a great price to live. This is why ancient achieved ones returned to nature. Nowadays, no one can live by the standards of ancient times with such freedom and peace. We all need to labor to support our lives materially, but with correct understanding, we can also further our cultivation at the same time. In this way, we do not work hard just for this lifetime; we work for something more lasting.

Physical death occurs when *chi* departs, so if you do not manage or control or refine your *chi*, then your physical life will be finished. The physical body is like a piece of wood. Unless a person cultivates oneself to change one's energy, once it is burned or used up, there will be nothing left but some bad-smelling smoke. It is important to nurture *chi* as the means of transcendence from physical to spiritual life. It is the middle point and the most important stage in spiritual self-cultivation. It cannot be neglected. Also, spirit should never be emphasized to the extent of neglecting *chi*. *Chi* is the foundation of silent cultivation and the most useful time to cultivate is now.

In spiritual cultivation we wish everyone would achieve spiritual purity, high mental quality and emotional independence. However, without natural *chi*, everything is empty and nothing can truly be realized. Also, without virtuous fulfillment, what is the value of your specially cultivated *chi*? In any practice, virtue is the basis and the cultivation of *chi* is next.

Cultivation Is a Life Path
In the spiritual world, there are many levels of spiritual achievement which need continual development, just as in

the human world. The levels closest to the human world are very low. For example, some spirits are not independent at all. Even though they are tiny and can live anywhere, they sometimes have the negative tendency to be parasitic. Their favorite targets are human beings. They can take advantage of all the labor and creation of humans, and often bring negative consequences to the "house" (body) and its "lord" (main soul). Some mental cases are not due to mental or emotional problems, but are caused by the possession of a ghost so there are two lords or bosses, or even more in the same house. The resulting inner conflict makes the person sick. Sometimes a spirit can suddenly become involved in the activities of a human being and cause them suffering, punishment or death. Their actions do not necessarily belong to the religious category of retribution, but rather to the consequences of the natural negative sphere finding expression in the human world.

Many people who have no spiritual ambition and are satisfied with only the physical and mental levels do not even know of spirits, but they still need spiritual self-protection. Some accidents and sickness are due to the interference of evil spirits that lead a person to suffer or be punished or killed. How can you guard yourself and be independent? The practices in this book can enhance one's personal spiritual strength and potential and keep away the attack of an unknown ghost.

Real independence is an achievement, not a gift. If you know the value of taking responsibility for yourself and if true independence is your goal, then you can engage in spiritual cultivation. Only by working through the stages of your development will you know more. That is why I offer the treasures of the ancient developed ones to people of high awareness. I will be happy when everyone achieves independence and becomes self-responsible.

Most spirits are not malevolent. Many people have been helped in their achievements in the human world by good spirits, but the spiritual world never takes credit for this. Humans always take the credit for all the great inventions and achievements, and ungratefully deny the existence of spirits. We can keep in mind that in the human world, anything involved with the body and mind of man and his affairs involves the spirits of man also.

The last thing I want to mention is that you must understand there is no way to escape the natural obligation of living, even though life is so burdensome at times. Once the life of a human being is established, a new spiritual universe is established. You have a great natural responsibility for your human life. You are a true god that sits in its center. You can never give up, you must guard and guide it well. This is how you continue a good life. There is no way to trade your own spiritual development for cheap religious salvation.

All spiritual achievement is a personal endeavor and not someone's charity to you. You find true life only through your own self-cultivation. Spiritual immortality only comes through your indefatigable cultivation and exploration. This accomplishment brings a true Heavenly paradise to you and to the people aroud you. If you live unnaturally, you will surely bring something different to yourself. Some people do not mind Heavenly blessings, but I do not think they welcome degradation, suffering and misery in their lives, so I hope everyone learns about a spiritual life and does not become too aggressive or make trouble for anyone else's spiritual cultivation.

I pass on what I received from the ancient spiritually achieved ones to those who will cherish and use it. My work in this stage is for those who wish to further their development. All of us need to fulfill our spiritual duty as human beings. We have received abundant gifts from the greatly achieved ones. I wish all of us have high appreciation for the gifts we receive from them. May we make them an inspiration for our own spiritual advancement.

Self-Development Involves Your Whole Life

A baby is an integral being; it is impossible to distinguish which part is the mind and which part is the spirit. The life of a newborn baby is that of a whole being, but after growing, disintegration can be seen in the body, emotions, sensations, desires, ambitions and all the various reactions to different sources. As a child develops mentally, it can think about spiritual matters, but it will no longer experience life as an integral whole. Why? Because the spiritual level is subtle and not everyone can understand or experience the true spiritual level.

If someone surpasses the doctrines of religion, it is an achievement, because most religious practices are like toys of human childhood. When most people mature, those things are no longer satisfying. All people have the innate right and knowledge to evaluate the truth of such things for themselves.

The true spiritual level of a human being is a kind of potential that is not always used. Some people do not value their spiritual potential and thus limit their life to only two spheres, the physical and the mental. In the case of people with high spiritual potential who do not develop it, it is like a wasted gift. Many educated or intellectual people also deny the existence of a spiritual level. This is a limitation and a sign of spiritual poverty. It happens because people are confused by shallow, artificial teachings which cloud the true value of spiritual life.

This book is for people who not only recognize the physical and mental spheres, but also recognize that they have spiritual potential and want to engage in spiritual cultivation. As a result of cultivation, they will redevelop their whole life being.

Our true spiritual being is not a single spiritual unity, but an entire spiritual universe. It is like a photograph of a person made up of many small dots. If each dot represents an entire human being, then these dots together form the larger picture. A developed human being is the composition of all the dots or entities. This analogy can be understood by the mind, but the mind alone can never reach the reality of truth. To truly reach the spiritual level depends on your own spiritual development.

The true, subtle body never dies. It is the consequence of the development of the spiritual potential of an ordinary human being. The ancient achieved ones knew how to use their spiritual potential, and through cultivation and continual development, they achieved themselves.

The basis of an ordinary body is many kinds of different cells. The cells make up organs, then systems, and finally a total being. The spiritual level is similar to the physical body. There are high spiritual entities, secondary spiritual entities, and basic spiritual entities of the physical level. The developed spiritual entities can be like you and can represent your total spiritual being. Any one of those small entities has obtained the whole essence of your being. Millions of spiritual lives can become you, and you can transform millions of spiritual lives with your single life being.

In doing your practice, those spiritual entities of your spiritual immortal being have numerical significance. One is valued as Oneness; two is valued as *yin* and *yang*; three is valued as the three spheres of Heaven, Man, and Earth; four is valued as the four groups of seven stars in the twenty-eight constellations; five is valued as the five elemental phases of universal energy; six is valued as the Six *Jia* (*yang*), and Six *Ding* (*yin*); seven is valued as the Big Dipper, and so forth. The ultimate metaphoric number is 36,000. This is the number of small spiritual entities that are organized as the oneness of you, an achieved immortal.

Practically speaking, when we are alive in the coarse level of the human sphere, all cultivation is supported by the physical level. In most people's cultivation, spirit is a late-comer in one way of speaking. God did not create the world, it is from the gross world that gods and goddesses are created.

If you achieve yourself after many years, you evolve to a different category of life. You evolve from the physical to the more subtle spiritual levels, and it is there you realize you are not the only spiritual being. There are many, many high spiritual beings. You have friends. You have a transcendental environment where happiness and enjoyment are free gifts derived from your inexhaustible spiritual life. It is a pity that many people limit themselves by their intellectual mind to only the physical and mental realms. Spiritual cultivation is a great enterprise. In human history there have not been many people who have achieved themselves, but the ways and the possibility have always been there. All people have a chance to cultivate and gather their personal spiritual potential.

After the physical body is deceased, some people transform to a non-conscious or partially conscious level, while others find eternal life in the spiritual realms. Everyone needs to be consciously self-responsible because life is a continuous process of evolution. If you are not evolving you will devolve and never reach the realm of eternal joy, or in ancient spiritual terms, the Three Realms of Great Purity. For people who have already reached this level and are still in worldly life, there is no more trouble or confusion because they know this level of life is only a game to play or duty to fulfill. Spiritually, I hope that each of you can achieve the level of the most spiritually wealthy. Then you will not mind if you win or lose the worldly game; it is all fun. It can all be gainful if you correctly and positively use your own worldly experience.

A Sage's Devotion

A sage who appears in the world
*   does not do so for his own sake.*
He responds to the troubled times of the world
*   out of his deep love for all people.*
He fulfills his moral nature by taking care of people
*   as he would his own children.*
He points out the right path for all people
*   by his responsible attitude.*
He loves to follow the wise teachings
*   of sages before him, so that the source of*
*   Heaven's support for people is uninterrupted.*
He does not value his own enjoyment
*   and neglect his mission in life.*
All people follow him happily,
*   yet this does not make him proud.*
He keeps his mind clear and undisturbed.
Like the bright, full moon his wisdom shines
*   upon the dark of night.*

(An ancient hymn about Chapter 49 of the *Tao Teh Ching.*

List of Practices

Index

To order: 800-578-9526 ✿ www.taostar.com:

Second Spring: Dr. Mao's Hundreds of Natural Secrets For Women to Revitalize and Rejunvenate at Any Age —This tip-filled guide for women shows how to enhance energy, sexuality and health, especially during the second half of life. Dr. Maoshing Ni invites women to fulfill their innate potential and be at their most vital, energetic and attractive.

#BSPR—264 pages, softcover. $17.99

The Complete Works of Lao Tzu—The *Tao Teh Ching* is one of the most widely translated and cherished works of literature. Its timeless wisdom provides a bridge to the subtle spiritual truth and assists you to live harmoniously and peacefully. Also included is the *Hua Hu Ching*, a later work by Lao Tzu which has been lost to the general public for a thousand years.

#BCOMP—212 pages, softcover. $13.95

Tao, the Subtle Universal Law—Most people are unaware that their thoughts and behavior evoke responses from the invisible net of universal energy. To lead a good and stable life is to be aware of the universal subtle law in every moment of our lives. This book presents practical methods that have been successfully used for centuries to accomplish this.

#BTAOS—208 pages, softcover. $16.95

I Ching, The Book of Changes and the Unchanging Truth—This legendary classic is recognized as the first written book of wisdom. Leaders and sages throughout history have consulted it as a trusted advisor for revealing the appropriate action in any circumstance. Includes over 200 pages of background material on natural energy cycles, as well as instruction and commentaries.

#BBOOK—669 pages, hardcover. $35.00

Attune Your Body with Dao-In—The ancients discovered that Dao-In exercises solved problems of stagnant energy, increased their health and lengthened their years. The exercises are also used as practical support for cultivation and higher achievements of spiritual immortality.

#BDAOI—144 pages, softcover. $16.95
Also on DVD. $24.95

Secrets of Longevity: Hundreds of Ways To Live To Be 100— Looking to live a longer, happier, healthier life? Try eating more blueberries, telling the truth, and saying no to undue burdens. Dr. Maoshing Ni brings together simple and unusual ways to live longer.

#BLON—320 pages, softcover. $14.95

Published by Chronicle Books

Secrets of Self-Healing—This landmark book on natural healing combines the wisdom of thousands of years of Eastern tradition with the best of modern medicine. Learn to treat common ailments with foods and herbs, and balance your mind and body to create vitality, wellness, and longevity.

#BSHEAL—576 pages. $16.95

Published by Penguin Group

The Tao of Nutrition—Chinese nutrition is flexible because it adapts to each individual's needs for the prevention or treatment of disease. Find over one hundred everyday foods along with their energetic properties and their usefulness in treating common conditions. A description of basic Chinese nutrition is included as well as meal plans and delicious recipes.

#BTAON —284 pages, softcover. $19.95

Sitting Moon: A Guide to Natural Rejuvenation After Pregnancy—Dr. Daoshing Ni and Jessica Chen, L.Ac., provide a four-week nutritional program that helps women reclaim their vitality after giving birth. Also discover how to create a support network and what supplies to have available. Become informed about post-labor physical changes and how to prevent illnesses by creating a foundation for emotional and spiritual well-being.

#BSITT—224 pages, softcover. $19.95

The Tao of Fertility: A Healing Chinese Medicine Program to Prepare Body, Mind, and Spirit for New Life—Dr. Daoshing Ni, an esteemed doctor who has helped countless women achieve their dream of having a child, offers his program for enhancing fertility through Traditional Chinese Medicine (TCM) and Taoist principles.

#BFERT—304 pages, softcover. $15.95 / Published by Collins

101 Vegetarian Delights—by Lily Chuang and Cathy McNease. From exotic flavorful feast to nutritious everyday meal, enjoy preparing these easy-to-make recipes. Based on the ancient Chinese tradition of balance and harmony, these dishes were created for the new or seasoned vegetarian. The desserts are truly delightful, and healthy as well.

#B101—176 pages, softcover. $15.95

Power of Natural Healing—Hua-Ching Ni discusses the natural capability of self-healing and presents methods of cultivation–practices that can assist any treatment method–which promote a healthy life, longevity, and spiritual achievement. There is a natural healing process inherent in the very nature of life itself. One's own spirit is the source of health.

#BHEAL—143 pages, softcover. $14.95

The Key to Good Fortune: Refining Your Spirit (Revised)—"Straighten your Way" (*Tai Shan Kan Yin Pien*) and "The Silent Way of Blessing" (*Yin Chi Wen*) are the main guidance for a mature, healthy life. Spiritual improvement can be an integral part of realizing a Heavenly life on earth.

#BKEY—153 pages, softcover. $17.95

8,000 Years of Wisdom, Volume I and II—This two-volume set contains a wealth of practical, down-to-earth advice given by Hua-Ching Ni. Drawing on his training in Traditional Chinese Medicine, herbology and acupuncture, Hua-Ching Ni gives candid answers to questions on many topics.

#BWIS1—Vol. I: (Revised edition)
            Includes dietary guidance. $18.50
#BWIS2—Vol. II: Sex and pregnancy guidance. $18.50

The Uncharted Voyage Toward the Subtle Light—This book provides a profound understanding and insight into the underlying heart of all paths of spiritual growth, the subtle origin, and the eternal truth of one universal life. Readers will enter a voyage of discovery, finding a fresh new light toward which to direct their life energy.

#BVOY—424 pages, softcover. $19.95

Instructional DVDs for Learning Tai Chi and Chi Gong

 **Self-Healing Qi Gong Meditation**—with Dr. Mao Shing Ni. The flow of qi (*chi*), or life force energy, is the basis of Chinese Medicine. Qi gong, a gentle movement practice, soothes the spirit, releases powerful healing energy, tones the body and enhances balance. Dr. Mao helps us understand the causes of disease and teaches techniques that can help relieve many common ailments.
#DSHCG—95 minutes, DVD, $29.95

 18-Step Harmony Style Tai Chi—with Dr. Mao Shing Ni. These easy-to-learn 18 movements form the basis of the 108-step Harmony Style Tai Chi form. Doing these 18 steps for a few moments every day can bring balance and gracefulness into your busy life. Tai chi also enhances vitality and strength.
#DSTEP—28 minutes, DVD, $24.95

 Attune Your Body with Dao-In—with Hua-Ching Ni. Dao-In is an ancient Taoist yoga that preceded tai chi and is practiced sitting and lying down. Despite its simplicity, it unlocks stagnant energy, increases strength and health, and calms the emotions. Includes self-massage and meditation.
#DDAOI—50 minutes, DVD, $24.95

CDs for Calming, Centering and Releasing

 Meditation for Stress Release—with Dr. Mao Shing Ni. Are you suffering from tension and anxiety? This body/mind qi gong meditation can bring you calming relief. Beginning with the guiding words of Dr. Mao, you can use awareness and visualization to find relaxation, tranquility and a restored spirit.
#CDSTRESS—26 minutes, CD, $12.95

 Invocations for Health, Longevity and Healing a Broken Heart—with Dr. Mao Shing Ni. Thinking is louder than thunder! Repeating these three magnificent Chinese invocations can help you achieve physical, emotional and spiritual health. The lush tones of the words are believed to have unique powers of their own. These invocations are a valuable inheritance from ancient China
#CDINVO—23 minutes, CD, $12.95

 Meditation for Pain Management—with Dr. Mao Shing Ni. Learn body/mind techniques used by martial artists and Taoist monks in intense training that enabled them to endure and transcend pain. Abandon limitations by outgrowing them. Overcome stiffness by mind-stretching your body. Learn visualization and meditation techniques that aid in the alleviation of pain.
#CDPAIN—22 minutes, CD, $12.95

Tao of Wellness, Inc.

1131 Wilshire Boulevard, Suite 300
Santa Monica, CA 90401
310-917-2200
www.taoofwellness.com

The Tao of Wellness center for Traditional Chinese Medicine is the integral way to total well-being and a long life. Each patient is seen as an individual whose health is immediately affected by his or her lifestyle including diet, habits, emotions, attitude, and environment. The center, co-founded by Drs. Daoshing and Mao Shing Ni, focuses on acupuncture and Chinese herbs to promote health, longevity, and fertility.

Wellness Newsletter:

View it and subscribe online at www.taoofwellness.com

Tao of Wellness Magazine:

Free subscription. Email name and address to: info@taostar.com

The Wellness Store

1412 Fourteenth Street
Santa Monica, CA 90404
310-260-0013
www.wellnesslivingstore.com
order@taostar.com

Herbs, books, tai chi and chi gong classes; healthy living products; public lectures; art gallery.

Tao of Wellness Herbs and Books
Yo San University Bookstore

13315 W. Washington Boulevard, Suite 200
Los Angeles, CA 90066
800-772-0222; 310-302-1207
www.taostar.com
info@taostar.com

A complete traditional Chinese medical university bookstore with a selection of medical books, acupuncture supplies and herbal supplements. Also available are tai chi and chi gong DVDs, meditation CDs to relieve stress, heal a broken heart or manage pain, books on Taoist teachings that nurture the spirit, and tools for positive living.

Yo San University of Traditional Chinese Medicine

13315 W. Washington Boulevard, 2nd floor
Los Angeles, CA 90066
877-967-2648; 310-577-3000
www.yosan.edu

One of the finest and most academically rigorous Traditional Chinese Medical schools in the United States, Yo San University offers a fully accredited Master's degree program in acupuncture, herbology, *tui na* body work, and chi (*qi*) movement arts. Students explore their spiritual growth as an integral part of learning the healing arts.

Yo San University Community Clinic

Lower-cost acupuncture and herbal medicine provided by supervised interns in their final phase of training at busy TCM practice. Treatment sessions with licensed acupuncturists are also available.

Yo San University Fertility Center

Have consultations and treatments by experienced doctoral-level acupuncturists who are doing residency in the nation's first-ever Clinical Doctoral Program in Oriental Reproductive Medicine.

Integral Way Society

PO Box 1530
Santa Monica, CA 90406-1530
310-577-3031 (voicemail)
info@taostar.com
www.integralway.org

Learn about natural spiritual teachings as transmitted by the Ni family through books, mentoring, and retreats organized by the mentors of the Integral Way. The IWS assists people in achieving physical, mental, spiritual, moral and financial health by nurturing self-respect and by offering methods of self-improvement based on the principles in the classic works of the *I Ching* and Lao Tzu's *Tao Teh Ching*.

Spiritual Self-Development: The Integral Way of Life

Internet study
info@taostudies.com
www.taostar.com

People who have read one or more books on the Integral Way of Life will find support in this study program. Having deepened their understanding and experience of the Way, students will learn how to live a constructive path of life.

College of Tao & Integral Health

Distance Learning Courses

Traditional Chinese Medicine Concepts of Chinese Nutrition
Includes DVD and course materials
15-45 CEU credits available
800-772-0222
taostar@taostar.com

Achieve a basic understanding of Chinese nutrition theories and its practical applications. In four illustrated manuals, topics covered are food energetics, Zang-Fu syndromes, diagnosis and nutrition counseling, food choices for specific illnesses, and patient education. Please contact us for a brochure.

Traditional Chinese Medicine (TCM) Studies
Includes audio CD, classroom notes, and all course materials
800-772-0222
taostar@taostar.com
www.collegeoftao.org

Listen to actual classroom lectures by exceptional instructors while having complete classroom notes for home study. May include reading and journal assignments, charts, textbooks, or raw herbs. Courses include:

Chinese Herbology
Traditional Chinese Medicine Theory: I, II, III
Chinese Acupuncture Points
Becoming a TCM Healer - 14 CEU credits
Power of Natural Healing - 14 CEU credits
Essence of Five Elements - 7 CEU credits
Bringing the Spirit to Your Healing Work
Traditional Chinese Medicine As Wellness Medicine
Introduction to Chinese Nutrition & Dietary Therapy
Public Health in America: A Study of the U.S. Healthcare System
Physiology of Disease Series: Global Disease Process
                              Organ Disease Process

Chi Health Institute

PO Box 2035
Santa Monica, CA 90406-2035
310-577-3031 (voicemail)
www.chihealth.org

The Chi Health Institute (CHI) offers professional education and certification in the Ni family *chi* movement arts including tai chi, chi gong, and Taoist meditation.

InfiniChi Institute International

PO Box 26712
San Jose, CA 95159-6712
408-295-5911
www.longevity-center.com/infinichi/infinichi.html,
or do a search for InfiniChi Institute International

Professional training in *chi* healing leads to certification as an InfiniChi practitioner. The program is designed to develop energetic healing abilities utilizing the Ni family books and texts that relate to Traditional Chinese Medicine, *chi gong*, Chinese bodywork, and natural spirituality. It features a progressive, systematic program that nurtures understanding, facilitates skill development, and promotes self-growth.

Acupuncture.com

www.acupuncture.com
800-772-0222
info@taostar.com

Acupuncture.com is the gateway to Chinese medicine, health, and wellness. From this site you can purchase Tao of Wellness herbal products, choose from a large selection of traditional formulas, and buy acupuncture books and related products.